OVERCOMING LEARNING
DIFFICULTIES

OVERCOMING

LEARNING

DIFFICULTIES

Edited by BOYD CROUCH

Secretary, School of Education
University of Reading

ERNEST BENN LIMITED/LONDON

First published by Ernest Benn Limited 1972
Bouverie House, Fleet Street, London EC4A 2DL

© *Ernest Benn Limited 1972*

Distributed in Canada by
The General Publishing Company Limited, Toronto

Distributed in the U.S.A. by
Lawrence Verry Inc., Mystic, Connecticut

Printed in Great Britain

ISBN 0 510-19610-1
Paperback 0 510-19611-X

Foreword

IT IS entirely coincidental that this note is being written the day after Mrs Thatcher's statement to the 1971 Conference of the NUT that some 350,000 children in secondary schools up and down the country are probably in need of special help.

In the chapters which follow it is hoped that teachers of both primary and secondary children and students will find a better understanding of why, under present conditions, so many children have difficulty in learning. They will also find practical suggestions for helping pupils not only in the basic subjects but also in those which give an opportunity for the development of creative ability. The two final chapters deal with the child in the home/school situation and in his personal relationships.

The contributors are all people who, in their different fields are concerned about and have been engaged in helping teachers of this type of child for a considerable time. That they represent such a wide spread of experience is not accidental, it springs from the conviction that the problems of the 350,000, and their successors, cannot be solved on a narrow front. In addition to selected experienced teachers, child rather than subject orientated, there is a great need for the involvement of people from many other services able and willing to discuss common problems and join in finding solutions to them.

Since the chapters comprising this book were written, the education of those mentally handicapped children whose needs cannot be met in ordinary schools has become the responsibility of the Education service. Consequently in September 1971, in addition to colleges already providing courses, six colleges of education began courses designed to train teachers for this special work. Another change planned to take place in 1974, with the reorganisation of the local authorities, is the combination of hospitals, general practitioners and the community health service in the establishment of assessment centres. This is an attempt to further the overall welfare of children handicapped by any factors which might impair learning. BOYD CROUCH

Contents

I

Physical Aspects of the Health of the Retarded Child

THERE ARE a number of questions which pose themselves to those concerned with any responsibility for the retarded child, as his problems are neither single nor simple. Amongst many needs relating to care and education is a general understanding of the physical aspects of the disability. These range from the fundamental question of cause of mental retardation to the associated effects linked with it. In addition to backwardness, the child's appearance and physique may be affected and much more frequently there may be disabilities of neurological function. The purpose of this chapter is to provide background information against which the problems of the mentally handicapped child can be recognized and understood as matters of personal and individual disability. In this way the child's difficulties, and those of the parents, can be known as a whole as well as in detail and the advice and education given is thus fully considered. A truism worth repeating is that to understand abnormality it is necessary to know what is normal. Accordingly this chapter first refers to normal processes and then considers some of the abnormalities which may affect the retarded child. Physical development must be studied concurrently with mental development for the whole assessment of the child but the latter is referred to separately elsewhere in this book.

PHYSICAL GROWTH AND GROWTH DISTURBANCE

Considerable interest in the phenomenon of growth has evolved in the last few years with developing techniques of measurement and improved statistical methods. There is now the opportunity to apply these to populations of children in this country and establish criteria of normality. For the simplest approach, measurement of height and weight is most used but it may be necessary to assess bodily proportions by linear and girth measurement. These and other refinements are needed in considering not just absolute growth but the changing pattern of growth which constitutes development and characterises maturity. To these standards of overall height and weight and definition of maturity is added the influence of individual variation in rate of development. A child may be constitutionally short or tall and yet mature early or he may exhibit a slower release of growth potential with delayed adolescence and continuing gain in height. It is necessary to evaluate these variations and in this we have been greatly assisted by Tanner in Great Britain, whose work has provided an understanding of the pattern of growth and a series of standards and methods of measurement for recording growth, the latter being of fundamental practical value. By applying these methods, measurement data are expressed in percentiles for age of the growing child. Thus, if an individual's height for age lies at the fiftieth percentile, this implies a mean position, with half the population being taller and the same number being shorter. An individual whose height for age is at the ninety-seventh percentile is only exceeded in height by three percent of the population of his age and is, therefore, very tall. Conversely, at the third percentile a person is particularly small. Nevertheless, in practice, this range, from third to ninety-seventh percentile, is regarded as representing a variation which is not abnormal. This approach, which is an alternative to expressing values as standard deviations, puts into perspective the individual record. The assessment of stature is dependent, clearly, only upon careful measurement and for full validity requires serial measurement, sometimes over years, to provide a picture of the pattern of growth. In this way a record may show both lag or catch-up as an indication of disease or health. Such measurement and type of percentile graph is usually applied to height, and to weight, the latter being a less reliable index of growth, but it may also be used to record adiposity by skin fold thickness, or bone growth as an important index of maturity by X-ray outline.

From a general view of the growing child, in terms of height and weight, it is possible to concentrate attention upon certain regions of the body and consider differential growth. Mediaeval portraiture of the infant failed to show this important process and depicted the baby as a diminutive adult. Now our observation accepts without comment the lengthening nose and upper lip of the rapidly maturing baby in the first few months of life so that even the mother's memory of the newborn is lost. The large head on small shoulders shrinks from a quarter to a seventh as a segment of overall length; the midpoint of the body ascends relatively as the legs lengthen with an eventual increase in trunk length. Body and facial contours change and change again. Puberty and sexual development is well documented. Knowledge of these aspects of development allows, once again, recognition of physical abnormality which is relatively uncommon, but is also the basis for informed reassurance as imagined disorder can cause emotional disturbance and concern in child and parent. Association between growth lack and intellectual retardation may exist in certain types of dwarfing. Growth failure with severe emotional stress is recognized, but the mechanism linking bodily growth and central nervous system function is understood only in outline and is probably not relevant to the general care of the retarded child. An aspect of regional or differential growth which is of importance is that of head size as measured by its horizontal circumference at forehead level with child looking forward. These measurements also lend themselves to percentile recording and where abnormally small they reflect failure of brain growth. Correlation between head size and intelligence is not significant within the normal range but the unduly small head of the child who is designated accordingly as microcephalic provides confirmation that all is not well. Disproportionately increased growth of the head and enlargement which can occur rapidly or slowly is also a certain sign of abnormality.

Growth, namely an increase in size and body cell number, and development, which represents differentiation of structure and function, combine to achieve maturity and the maximum of stature which we regard as the adult state. This theoretically concludes the phase of growing up and heralds senescence. The pattern and pace of increase and differentiation is specific to man from the moment of conception when it is determined by the inherited genetic constitution of the individual. Thereafter this potential is promoted to follow a predetermined course or is modified by innate flaw or subsequent injury or deprivation. Examples of these adverse influences are infrequent and only occasionally will they appear in any group of retarded children. Nevertheless it is important that every disability should be considered and any small and retarded child should be assessed physically in order to identify a possible reason for altered stature.

It is convenient to adapt Sheridan's categories of risk of handicap, for the purpose of considering the causes common to physical and mental retardation.

1. *Background Group*. Those in which a constitutional factor is responsible. Because the individual characteristic of stature is ordinarily multifactorial in a genetic sense there may be no impressive familial or racial influence, even if detail of the pedigree is known. It is therefore unlikely that inheritance will contribute recognisably to individuals who are retarded in intellectual development and who are also physically exceptionally small, although there are examples of this which might lie in rare familial metabolic disorders. Included in this group is chromosome abnormality, such as mongolism. Here the defect lies in the preparation of the ovum for conception and among the characteristic features of this common syndrome is that of small stature.

2. *Prenatal Group*. The foetus is remarkably well protected in pregnancy but during the period of intense and complicated development in the first three months it is crucially susceptible to the German measles virus derived from its mother. The virus continues to inhabit the foetus until well after birth and in doing so stunts growth, probably lastingly, as well as sometimes harming the development of heart, brain and eye. Other prenatal factors are less recognised but in certain low birth-weight babies inhibition both of general growth and cerebral development may be due to a common factor operating from early pregnancy. Although a proportion of other very low birth-weight babies show a much increased risk of brain impairment, they are much less likely to remain physically small than the first group of so-called low birth-weight dwarfs. Organs other than the brain may show abnormal formation in early pregnancy: for example, the heart and kidneys may be so severely deformed as to impair growth in childhood. However, this carries no increased risk of mental retardation, although special educational need may be required for the deprivations of prolonged invalidism.

3. *Perinatal Group*. Although the mechanism of infant birth and the establishment of independent life presents great potential risk to the baby, there is no direct interference with growth.

4. *Postnatal and Later Childhood Group*. In these children some major disturbance comes to light in childhood and interferes with growth. This may represent a failure of the organs which control growth by internal secretion of chemical substances: the pituitary

gland, the thyroid gland and the suprarenal gland. There may be delayed loss of reserve function by disease or malformation of a major organ such as heart, kidney or lungs and growth may be arrested. Nutrition may fail because of severe deprivation or gastro-intestinal disease or some chronic infection may persist and stunt the child. Backward children are more prone to the risk of infection. By their behaviour and feeding difficulties their nutrition may be impaired. A small group of neurological disorders in childhood result from abnormal biochemical metabolism which may or may not be treated by a selective diet. These inevitably interfere with overall growth as they operate from birth, but they may not be apparent until later infancy and childhood despite improved methods of biochemical screening after birth. Otherwise in this group the handicap is seldom one of intellect and stunting. Often there is an important educational need nevertheless, determined by impaired health and loss of formal schooling.

The changes of growth and development present an added dimension to the life and needs of the child. No attempt has been made here to describe them as such and there are many detailed publications on the subject. Instead an endeavour has been made to outline the processes of growth, rather than the precise pattern, and to indicate where the impairment of these processes is shared with those of the brain.

THE CAUSATION OF MENTAL RETARDATION

As with any serious illness or handicap it is natural to seek an explanation of the cause. In the case of mental retardation there is a variety of recognised abnormalities which may cause impairment of brain function and so interfere with intelligence. Nevertheless it is seldom possible to identify a specific factor in a given case and in our ignorance we tend to ascribe retardation to faulty development of the brain, to mis-called cerebral *agenesis*, to cerebral dysfunction, to primary retardation and so on, in terms which are speculative and perhaps misleading. Every effort should be made, as soon as possible, to exclude a demonstrable cause by medical examination and laboratory tests once the fact of developmental delay and the purpose of investigation is explained to the parents. The object of investigation is to find a correctible cause for the condition and so to remedy the situation. Unfortunately this is only very rarely feasible but is of some reassurance to know that the matter has been explored as fully as possible. Secondly, if a cause that is untreatable but recognisable can be identified, counselling is indicated to advise on the risk of recurrence so that appropriate guidance can be given to prevent a similar event. If no cause can be determined, then more empirical advice has to be considered and offered on the basis of the fullest information possible, as guidance also to the risk of recurrence. For these reasons alone it is necessary to discuss the problem with the child's parents at the earliest stage at which retardation can unequivocally be confirmed. If the certainty of retardation is in doubt, the timing of discussion and explanation must depend upon judgement of the doctor concerned but in general there is everything to be gained by early and frank explanation to resolve uncertainty where possible and accept it when necessary. If no cause can be found, this must be explained and the matter left open but not obscured by uncertainties which lead to regret, doubt and recrimination. It is especially wrong to hint at difficulties at the birth of the child when these may be unconfirmed; and even if confirmation is certain, confident correlation between birth difficulty and brain impairment is seldom possible and usually injudicious and unhelpful.

The causes of mental retardation may be considered under the headings already noted with regard to physical growth defect.

1. *Background Group.* Here the recognizable basis may be assigned to genetic influence or chromosomal disorder. At this point may it be stated that explanation of these mechanisms is regarded as beyond the scope of this chapter. Nevertheless it is of importance that some knowledge should be sought of the simple mechanisms of inheritance and the basic facts of cytogenetics which for the uninitiated are less daunting and much more interesting than they sound. Several clear and popular texts are available. Intelligence as influenced by gene function may be modified by multiple gene action in a blending effect of genetic factors from either parent. Endowment from parents of low intelligence will transmit genes governing a similar characteristic. On rarer occasions one gene may produce a dominant effect which emerges to some degree to cause physical tissue abnormality which interferes with the brain. The fibrous tumours situated within the brain and on the skin in the syndrome of tuberose sclerosis or epiloia are an example of this type of condition. Less infrequently a corresponding gene from each parent may reinforce its hitherto latent effect in the pattern of

recessive inheritance. This usually corresponds with a specific biochemical effect of enzyme failure – a block in a crucial biochemical pathway causes accumulation of an unmetabolised substance, the detection of which in body fluids provides the diagnosis. At the same time the biochemical disorder is toxic in its effect on the brain. Such is the case in phenylketonuria recognised in 1934 and tested for today in every newborn infant because it can be controlled by dietary means in which the precursor of the toxic metabolite is eliminated from the diet. There are several similar conditions in which dietary control is much less rewarding.

The majority of genes do not influence cerebral function but where grouping of considerable multiples of genes becomes distorted at a grosser level there is an inevitable and more subtle effect on many body structures which also involves the brain on a more general scale. Such is the case in chromosome disturbance. It is estimated that about one percent of live born children have some serious chromosome disorder. The majority of these involve chromosome number with additional unit of chromosome material in every cell nucleus. Approximately half involve the pair of chromosomes governing sexual differentiation, and mental retardation is a variable feature; disturbance of the other half affects one of the remaining chromosomes referred to as an autosomal without influence on sexual characteristics. An example of this lies in the common and familiar form of defect known as mongolism or Down's syndrome.

2. *Prenatal Group.* In these children there is a recognised or assumed insult to the developing or growing brain. German measles and accidental over-exposure to ionising radiation provide recent and past examples of this aetiology. Later on in pregnancy the foetus is no longer susceptible to deformity of the brain because its structure is established. But it is susceptible to disease which, as in postnatal life, may cause inflammation and damage and such may arise, although rarely from virus or protozoal infection derived from the mother. As in the case of growth impairment attributed to prenatal influences, evidence of specific harm to the brain from other causes is not proved although abnormality of the uterus may play a part. These rather restricted influences allow one to discount and give reassurance on the many imagined or traditional influences in pregnancy which may harm the baby.

3. *Perinatal Group.* This term refers to the time interval at the end of pregnancy when premature labour may bring forth a viable baby

and includes the first week of infant life. Thus, it covers a continuum in which the preparation of the baby for birth and its actual birth and recovery therefrom are the paramount factors. Factors which render the infant susceptible to cerebral risk lie in depletion of body store of sugar at a time when fall in blood sugar level is particularly harmful and difficult to detect – the brain being dependent on a satisfactory level and damaged by lack. There is the associated fragility of the brain due to prematurity with the possibility of haemorrhage. The resilience of the full term infant in sustaining temporary interruption of oxygen supply is not yet acquired and is at added risk from breathing difficulties. Thus, the baby who is born early or whose nutrition has been limited before birth, is at a particular risk, which may persist until growth has achieved stability of function. To these risks are added those which may affect any newborn infant, but it is very difficult to apportion them retrospectively in a subsequently retarded baby. So many infants suffer some or all of these difficulties unscathed that additional vulnerability is postulated to explain hazard of birth or low birth-weight. This weakness may rise in earlier pregnancy and render the infant more at risk than from the direct effect of later birth difficulty. Thus, it is proper, as mentioned, not to emphasise the complications of the perinatal period as cause for retardation when there may be underlying and unknown factors. None the less, there is considerable likelihood of handicap in the very low birth-weight baby.

4. *Postnatal and Later Childhood Group.* Here the cause of brain abnormality may be strictly acquired in terms of physical accidental injury or infective disease such as meningitis or encephalitis. Alternatively it may become apparent as a result of innate disturbance of a constitutional kind as mentioned with biochemical or other disorder, including degenerative processes which develop at any time. Structural abnormality of the brain, causing dilation with cerebro-spinal fluid, so-called hydrocephalus, may be another factor.

The recognition of retardation is commonly achieved by failure of the baby to reach an expected milestone of development and appreciation of this will depend upon the experience of the parent. Delay in sitting, walking or talking may draw attention to the problem but abnormal feeding difficulty or behaviour such as continued crying can arouse concern. All these difficulties may have other causes and their evaluation requires care and a sense of responsibility. The earlier the diagnosis of retardation is reached the better, but full evaluation requires observation, investigation, counselling and parental support, and this multiple approach necessitates both time and coordination. The family doctor, community health services and hospital all have a part to play. To mount this by design, as it were, and to achieve recognition of handicap, the concept of a Risk Register was introduced. Thus, all infants whose history, before and after birth, suggested abnormality may be listed on a community basis and subjected to the machinery of particular diagnostic scrutiny and follow up. Unfortunately it has been found that a high proportion of infants not on the Register have developed with a handicap and that many designated at risk have developed normally. Thus, it may be better to be more selective of a particularly high risk group and devote resources to wider, but necessarily less frequent diagnostic screening to cover the infant and pre-school population as a whole. At the same time it has been advocated that assessment and diagnostic services be grouped to provide expertise and advice on an area and regional basis so that full identification of handicap is achieved.

Assessment of the child cannot be conducted too early provided that it is carried out by a person trained in developmental testing and the interpretation and identification of disability. In this country, Illingworth has pioneered the study of, and written very widely about the assessment of development with emphasis on its predictive value. Testing is essentially that of function in various capacities and the special senses of hearing and sight need particular attention. More recently the importance of testing in the newborn period has been emphasised with regard both to prediction and to judgement of maturity of the neonatal nervous system. This approach, when combined with improved biochemical screening for inborn errors of metabolism, will constitute the initial stage of the general pattern of scrutiny of all children, to be carried out with tact and explanation.

From the preceding discussion of the several causes of mental subnormality and the association between this handicap and disordered somatic growth it may be assumed perhaps that developmental delay and lowered intelligence constitute the sole outcome of brain impairment. Unfortunately, subnormality is not the only manifestation, and this is to be expected when the multiplicity of brain function is considered. In addition to intellectual loss, or more precisely, failure of intellectual gain, there are other main disabilities with which retardation is often, although by no means always, associated. Amongst these are cerebral palsy and epilepsy. The first represents primarily a continued disturbance of movement and the second shows phasic, systematised but quite irrelevant, uncontrolled function of the brain. Further, there may be additional disorders of the central reception and comprehension of sound by the brain and a comparable impairment of vision and body awareness. Finally the picture may be dominated by gross disturbance of behaviour. This may take the form, in the most disabled child, of expression reduced to the simplest repetitive movements, or conversely, to a ceaseless destructive hyperactivity which eventually subsides. A third pattern is that of the completely withdrawn bizarre picture of childhood autism. From this spectrum of disorder only that of cerebral palsy and epilepsy will be considered. The first of these affects about two children in every thousand born and the second about twice as many.

Multiple Handicap and Cerebral Dysfunction

It has been mentioned that, with the complex structure of the nervous system and diffused effect of any insult to the brain, a disability seldom involves just one particular function. This is illustrated by the pattern of an epileptic seizure. Occasionally it may be focal in its effect and cause only the jerking of a limb or, in *petit mal* attacks, a transient lapse of consciousness; but usually there is distortion or disturbance of sensation, awareness, movement and visceral function. All capacities of the brain briefly disintegrate. Where there is lasting but lesser disorder, as in cerebral palsy, the influence of injury or maldevelopment is also widely distributed. The main weakness is one of movement but there is likely also to be a definite risk of impaired vision, of deafness, of speech defect, of altered awareness of the body image and of intellectual disability – all as an expression of disturbed function.

Thus it is insufficient to attend to the primary handicap and ignore the possibilities of other disability. Full assessment of these requires much expertise and evaluation by several clinical and educational disciplines. To achieve this, the establishment of a team of experts is needed for diagnosis and to maintain review. This approach, which is essential, is being formalised in the setting up of Assessment Centres recommended by the Department of Health and Social Security to be on an area and regional basis in association with hospital departments concerned with children.

There are many children who draw attention to themselves by showing to a slight degree one or more of the disabilities mentioned. This may be in the form of limited progress at school with learning difficulties or an observant teacher may notice undue clumsiness or a tendency to minor injury. Emotional disturbance may present an acute situation or there may be a less striking general immaturity of behaviour. Sadly, they may never be noticed at all. For these children the designation 'Minimal Cerebral Dysfunction' has been given. A pompous neologism, but one to indicate the importance of such a group. It represents the end of a spectrum of disability which may be scarcely perceptible but which grades to definite recognition of obvious disorder. At one end of the scale there may simply be clumsiness, at the other very severe cerebral palsy with multiple handicap and gross disability.

Spina Bifida and Meningomyelocoele
This condition is one in which the infant is born with its lower spinal cord exposed on the surface of the back. This results in damage to the nerves leaving that level of the cord and there is greater or lesser degree of paralysis of the legs, the bladder and the sphincter muscle controlling the continence of the bowel. A corresponding area of loss of sensation is associated. Combined with this defect almost always is an abnormality of the base of the brain which blocks the flow of fluid within it and gradually distends and thins out brain substances. If untreated this causes gross subnormality and blindness in extreme cases. The handicap is multiple, with paralysis of the legs, impairment of intelligence and a form of bladder paralysis which leads to kidney damage. Surgical treatment can prevent significant brain damage and reduce the extent of the motor weakness. Attention to the bladder can greatly lessen the risk of lethal kidney involvement. Thus combined surgical treatment, often spaced over several years, can reduce the handicap considerably and wherever feasible, a team approach from infancy to adolescence is essential. This imposes much parental strain but operative treatment achieves vast improvement. This involves the newborn where immediate attention is needed but continued care and education are subsequently also necessary throughout life. Despite this the early mortality is high and we do not know the eventual outlook for all these children.

The incidence of this abnormality is between 2 and 3 per thousand and so it corresponds closely to that of cerebral palsy. As in cerebral palsy there is a major proportion of mental handicap with marked physical disability. A prolonged programme of treatment is required and considerable resources and expenditure are involved in what is now a national commitment. These children will require an increasing proportion of special school facilities. As in so many congenital abnormalities the cause is unknown but with a racial and familiar element and varied geographical distribution. No means of prevention, therefore, is known.

The Deprivation Syndrome
When stimulation is lacking considerable delay in certain fields of development may result. This is noticeable in some residential and fostering care when motor and speech delay are present, with subsequent recovery. It may be more marked in retarded children who are ignored and whose limited potential is not promoted. Absence of affection leads to emotional disturbance and it is necessary to consider the background situation in any handicap which may be aggravated and conditioned by the environment.

The Sensory Handicaps
These represent a much smaller incidence of handicap than that of subnormality, epilepsy or cerebral palsy and comprise blindness and deafness. The number of blind and partially sighted children in England and Wales probably does not exceed 5,000 and severe deafness affects one child in 1,000. It takes little consideration to remind us of the dimension of the handicap of blindness or deafness in an adult but in the child with the deprivation of the stimulus of the major senses on the whole process of development the disturbance is more fundamental.

There is no particular pattern of intelligence linked either to blindness or deafness but where the origin is prenatal or perinatal there is more likely to be a neurological deficit as well. German measles, harming the developing foetus, may cause deafness, dullness and severe eye involvement. Deafness may result from brain scarring by severe jaundice which can arise just after birth and this may affect intelligence. Extreme prematurity may contribute to central brain impairment as we know, and also to the risk of damage to the retina. The more global disturbance causing a cerebral palsy or severe retardation may interrupt visual nerve fibre tracts within the brain and so restrict the field of vision. These are all examples of the major causes of combined handicap but more frequently blindness or deafness occurs separately from isolated sensorineural failure, without identifiable cause and there are no means yet of prevention.

Because of the profound effect of neurodevelopmental progress the recognition of these disabilities at the earliest possible moment is of extreme importance. From the parents' point of view they can adjust and come to terms with disability as early as possible without protracted doubt. The evolution of the handicap can be better understood and anticipated the earlier it is recognised and the better and less prejudiced the family relationship. For the child appropriate treatment can be given as soon as possible, full assessment of potential is established early, and, of the greatest importance, the management of the child can be guided as expertly as possible to provide warm and balanced care with stimulation without pressure, consistency without rigidity and security without overprotection. Simple observation and testing can achieve diagnosis in the early months of life where the defect is profound. When this is partial it may be unnecessarily delayed into later childhood.

Other Physical Disorders

The majority of long-standing problems in childhood are fortunately less severe and distressing. Nevertheless, there are many with some impact on learning, emotional adjustment or school attendance and these require some consideration. It is not possible to classify them except broadly by body systems.

Stature

The small child is a cause for concern partly from sheer physical hazard in a boisterous and at times heartless school community. Almost always his small stature is constitutional and not an indication of ill health but it is important to observe stature measurement, assign a percentile and investigate significant lag.

The tall child presents no problem as a rule in this society with its secular trend to earlier maturity. Temporary psychological disturbance may result from embarrassment of disproportionate tallness, but this is lost when precocity is followed by maturity.

The fat child is a common problem in these days of relative affluence and some two percent of the school population may now be affected. The condition is essentially one of excess food intake for the particular need of the individual. A constitutional tendency to obesity is recognised, but is not glandular in the sense of endocrine disturbance, and family eating habits predominate as the usual cause of gluttony and seemingly inherited overweight. Emotional disturbance may provoke over-eating as solace and compensation but this is unusual primarily. Treatment can only be effective by the rigid adherence to a strict diet and where doctors fail, the ritual of weight-watching groups often succeeds. However, the prognosis is generally poor and fat children become overweight adults with a potential limitation of life expectancy. Nevertheless, it is the responsibility of all in authority to achieve a cure for this preventable condition by seeking advice and by appropriate action.

Respiratory Disorders

Fortunately these cause little morbidity. Asthma, however, affects between two and three percent of the childhood population and disability and absenteeism from school may be marked. The condition is essentially a breathing difficulty caused by constriction of the air-way tubes into the lungs. This is provoked by infection showing as bronchitis, although more usually an asthmatic spasm is caused by an allergy or hypersensitivity to inhalants. Recent drug therapy has much improved the outlook in this condition which usually persists through childhood into adolescence and then diminishes.

Alimentary Disorder

Recurrent abdominal pain is a common symptom in young children of the middle years. Seldom is it organic in origin and it is accepted that the majority of incidents of pain have an innocent basis with spontaneous recovery. Acute bouts of pain necessitate medical attention nevertheless, because of the risk of appendicitis in the parents' mind as well as in actuality. Investigation is seldom rewarding but is necessary in the severe or recurrent cause to assess the possibility of a psychogenic element and rule out a curable condition.

Renal

Urinary tract infection is more common than recognised. It is recurrent and may cause loss of schooling. There is evidence that it may be latent in some five percent of the schoolgirl population. Its importance lies in a small risk of long-term renal harm so that it should always be investigated and treated with careful follow-up observation.

Conclusion

All the disabilities mentioned have one factor in common, namely the loss of educational opportunity for the child either by his inability to learn or by the distress and absenteeism of illness. It is our obligation to understand, in the fullest detail possible, the extent of this deprivation and to remedy it by every means.

2

Learning and Learning Disorder

INTRODUCTION

WATCHING A normal young infant exploring his environment it is easy to see that his primitive learning consists of a blending of activities. He learns *to* and he learns *that*. He learns *to* coordinate his muscular function. He learns *that* sounds occur, *that* light strikes his eyes, *that* things taste sweet or sour, *that* temperatures or pressures can cause a variety of stages of comfort and discomfort. If the infant is seriously ill or grossly immature the extent and quality of learning is severely modified. The simplest description of such a situation which we hear is that the infant 'hasn't the energy to learn', or, 'is too busy surviving'. Though superficially simple, these two descriptions hold considerable significance. We all recognise that producing change demands creation and release of energy. We all recognise that the release of energy must be directed towards the particular change which is required. The simple laws of mechanics remind us of such phenomena as inertia, friction and the conservation of energy, all of which relate to the problems of movement or change. All learning involves a change of state. The first steps demand the initiation of coding processes. In order to teach – or to create situations in which learning can occur – we are bound by the criteria underlying change of any kind. In other words, before beginning to consider the avenues through which learning can occur we need to think of those elements which relate most cogently to change.

Learning at the rate which occurs in the first two years of life requires large quantities of energy, a focusing of attention, normal sensory inputs, an adequate amount of intelligence and, particularly, an environment which is conducive to their most effective deployment. We can, therefore, say that the infant learns *from, to* and *that*! One tends to think of early learning as a complicated storage function, which in fact it is. But learning is also an expenditure of energy, a developing perceptual and attentive skill and either depends on, stems from or leads towards a rapid sequence of emotional learning, maturation and gratification. Gratification may arise from what is learned, for instance, that this is the source of food or of comfort, or of security and love. Achievement of learning, for example, the recognition that a problem has been solved or that curiosity is satisfied may be a source of gratification. But such gratifications play only a minor part; a major source of gratification and maturation is the child's own recognition of the *fact of* learning, not so much *what* he has learned but *that* he has learned. One of the most important aspects of knowledge is the awareness that we know. The use of knowledge is facilitated by awareness of its extent and depth but, more important, it is facilitated by recognition that a problem exists, that the problem can possibly be solved, and by some assurance that we hold the solution to it. Such an attitude is not simply a facet of recall because the observer must focus his perceptual skills on the stimulus object or situation before recall can occur. Focusing demands attention; it is based on a prior state of self-regard in which the observer is aware of his skills and his knowledge and has the confidence which is one aspect of the positive reinforcement produced by success. Successful learning is merely one link in the chain. Positive reinforcement is commonly recognised as a result of successful learning; it is less commonly recognised as a reinforcement of the total learning process. Throughout this chapter the ideas outlined above are extended to the consideration of the psychological development of the child in so far as it leads to or is affected by problems of learning.

INFORMATION SYSTEMS

Although learning is based on the senses and their proper coordination there is a danger of over-emphasising the importance of this fact. The processes by which the brain coordinates sensory information are at least as vulnerable to stress and disorder as are the senses themselves. It is thus necessary to consider the following processes when thinking of potential learning problems.

1. Perceptual discrimination
2. Conceptual thinking
3. Remembering
4. Reasoning
5. Imagining

These classes are part of the process by which we use the senses to obtain information, to store and organise it, to develop it as the basis for ideas or concepts. The same processes facilitate the testing and ratification of concepts or hypotheses and eventually lead to the formulation of continuous thought processes. The expression of these normally leads to their confirmation, modification or correction and hence it is important to remember that the reasoning processes require expressive as well as receptive functions. Assessment of sensory acuity has now developed into a considerable science but all who work in such fields recognise that acuity is only one aspect of the total sensory process. To illustrate this we need only consider the difference between hearing and listening. Hearing is commonly defined as 'detection of sound by the ear and its transmission to the primary auditory area of the cortex'. One definition of listening is 'the ability to attend to heard sound with the object of interpreting its significance.' Consideration of the latter definition will remind us that the classroom situation is rarely, if ever, concerned with hearing in its strict sense. We are concerned with listening and hence with auditory attention. As soon as we begin to consider those factors which modify auditory attention we are led back to those aspects of discrimination which, even at the auditory level, require remembering, some reasoning and hence a considerable degree of conceptualisation. The clinician recognises that a mild degree of auditory impairment is commonly associated with a major degree of auditory inattention and that failures of discrimination which lead to error not only undermine confidence but also inhibit and modify recall. Such modification will inevitably introduce delays and impair the whole process of remembering. To distil the whole massive literature on *remembering* into a few sentences is obviously impossible but we can perhaps consider certain of the memory processes in so far as they relate to the problems of learning disorder. At a very simple level we may say that remembering demands a stimulus object or situation which, when perceived by the observer, is related to prior experience and from this relationship some aspect of recall occurs. In thinking of this we can see that the organisation of attention demands a skill in two different directions simultaneously. One feature of attention is focused on the stimulus, the other on the stored codes of previous experience. Following the establishment of some quality of relationship between these events, recall normally occurs. The important point here is that recall demands the ability to maintain this kind of split-level attention, hence in those cases where duration of attention is limited we may expect problems of recall. Recall delays will lead to loss of confidence, leading to loss of attention and so the vicious circle commences. It is important, therefore, to remember that even relatively brief periods of loss of acuity lead to loss of auditory attention and that this commonly persists for a considerable period after hearing has returned to normal. Since it is quite common for certain mild hearing losses to fluctuate for prolonged periods the effect on attention, and therefore discrimination, should be kept in mind. The child with an almost minimal hearing loss (undetectable without specialized facilities) when seated at the back of the class, loses attention and discrimination which can have the same effect as a much more severe loss. In fact, research in the Royal Berkshire Hospital Audiology Unit has shown that if the child with a 20 db loss is given a speech test while seated at the back of the class, he tends to score as though he has a 60 db loss (for which a hearing aid is normally supplied). This cannot simply be attributed to attenuation of sound-pressure level due to distance but rather to the effects of attention loss and the intrusion of classroom noise between speaker and listener. Mild degrees of visual impairment may be expected to produce similar consequences. The spectacle-wearer, deprived of spectacles, sometimes requires a prolonged period of attention-focus before he can begin to use his impaired vision to its best effect. The consequences of undetected visual impairment which used to merit special mention in Teacher Training Colleges between the wars are still as severe, though happily their occurrence is now considerably less common. However, the results of improved testing facilities may have led us to a state of misplaced euphoria due to the emphasis placed on acuity rather than perception or discrimination (see below).

Reasoning was the fourth process mentioned which involves the senses and the brain. This may be described as the application of the cognitive processes to past experience in order to deal with present problems or to plan for the future. It is compounded *inter alia* from the following:

(a) Intelligence
(b) Personality
(c) Physical health (which includes normality of sensory and neurological functions)

(a) *Intelligence*

Although psychologists recognise that the prognostic value of intelligence testing is considerably less reliable than used to be thought, there is still quite a demand throughout society for such scores. The faulty notion of their accuracy and reliability leads to their continued usage even amongst informed people (cf. Mensa, the organisation for that proportion of the population who score highly on test).

Many selection procedures used by banks, the Armed Forces and many educational systems are based on the old idea that in one brief period the applicant can produce a pattern of success which is a consistent and reliable index of future performance. When it is remembered that many intelligence tests demand visual and auditory perception or perhaps reading skill, it is obvious that, particularly in group situations, a candidate may well fail an intelligence test which never gets past the perceptual level. The same comment is, of course, true in the classroom. How many children who make poor reading progress are ever given tests of visual or auditory perception, discrimination, or short-term memory?

Educationists agree that it is not possible to define intelligence but there the agreement ends. Hence, the following description of intelligence represents no more than a personal preference from those available. Intelligence is sometimes described as a name given to the overall efficiency and level of complexity of an individual's cognitive processes. Whether one agrees with Hebb's Theory of Intelligence or not, his description of its availability to test merits attention. He postulates three levels of intelligence. The first, or genetic potential level, he grades A and says that it is non-observable and non-measurable. The observed product in the individual's behaviour between the environment and the genetic potential he describes as Intelligence B. His final distinction is between observed and measured intelligence. This is simply a sample of B scored in intelligence quotients or other units. Since this sampling involves myriads of features ranging from genetic to environmental features on the one hand or from linguistic to perceptual features on the other it is clear that consistency and reliability are, to say the least, vulnerable. Now that children are no longer to be excluded from education on the basis of such sampling (or placed in an environment which would effectively prevent the child from ever disproving the original label) we may feel that reliance on intelligence test scores is no longer a serious matter. However, the challenge to education posed by children with learning disorders poses severe problems of assessment which have not yet been met satisfactorily. Fortunately, we are now sufficiently aware of the importance of interaction between the individual and the environment to encourage educational research into optimal environments and perhaps into levels of specific learning disorder which have not yet progressed much further than the psychological laboratories.

(b) *Personality*

When we turn to personality features the situation can become unbearably complex. Fortunately, most teachers spend a large part of their professional life either consciously or unconsciously observing and adapting to the personalities of children and so it is feasible to select and specify certain particular elements. We accept that the total social environment has a predictable function. (Bernstein has related this to the level of linguistic development.) We also accept that the social environment of the home has considerable significance. Many claim that the school itself provides another social environment and there is general agreement that at least two, and often three of these, can permanently affect the full maturation of personality. Although concerned more with academic progress than personality, the work of researchers underlines the relevance of a stimulating environment to learning. (The recent award of a RIBA medal to a deaf architect for his design of a school for deaf children which emphasized environmental stimulation is an interesting example of the acceptance of such ideas.) One suspects that many teachers might harbour the wry suspicion that environments may, from time to time, be too stimulating! There is no doubt of the truth of this judgement in the case of children with impaired ability to attend or who are hyperdistractable. Some classrooms which are designed for the child without problems are intolerably distracting for a significant proportion of our children. Since hyperdistractability is not merely a function of low levels of intelligence we could well ask ourselves whether the carefully controlled visual conditions of a language laboratory could not be extended to other educational activities. The same comments apply with equal force to auditory distractions. One does not need to live near to London's Heathrow Airport to be aware of the intrusive effect of noise, but there is still room for more specific research into controlled auditory environment for education, particularly when learning disorders pose additional problems.

Physical Health

The above comments lead us to consider the third element of reasoning outlined on p. 27. When one talks of the health or functional normality of the child such factors as nutrition and illness are of course, relevant, particularly when they lead to any danger of under-functioning or of time lost in school. Other factors at least equally important deserve special emphasis in this book. These relate to the general, physical, psychological and emotional well-being of the child. Most teachers have had experience of the child who suddenly flags, is given to mysterious loss of energy or who needs periods of rest, particularly in the primary school. Are we always right to blame this on too much television or too little sleep? What of the 'clumsy' child who cannot kick a ball, does not learn to write to our satisfaction as quickly as the rest of the class, is constantly bumping into things in class or requiring first aid in the playground? How many of our class children are severely enuretic? How many children appear to be able to maintain auditory attention but find visual attention unbearable? How many more are 'as good as gold with a book in their hands' but disturb the rest of the class when auditory attention is required? Our present levels of provision are quite inadequate for such children. The School Health Service has concentrated for many years on ensuring that all children undergo a regular, though necessarily rather superficial, investigation. Many authorities are now paying increasing attention to 'problem children' but it will be many years before medical research will really be able to come to grips with these specialised problems of educational paediatrics.

TEACHERS' ROLE

The inclusion in this book of a chapter on Pastoral Care is evidence of the awareness of the need to establish and maintain good working relationships between home and school. The teacher of the child with learning problems needs to know the parents, to be able to offer some means of developing the kind of close relationship in which mutual respect and confidence can grow. Domestic problems are one of the major sources of stress on the children in our care and the bewildered, frustrated, aggressive or apathetic states we see (to name but a few) often stem from family relationships which are not conducive to the emotional well-being of the child. We will not really come to grips with these in the busy heartiness of a parent-teacher meeting, yet the arrangement of special interview facilities at school is often difficult or artificial. There is much to be said for home visits which, in the case of deaf children, are recognised as part of the professional function of teachers and are accepted by parents and teachers alike. There is a lot to be said for meeting parents on their home ground. This is not simply because insights are to be gained from seeing the domestic conditions in which the pupil lives but also because the teacher who visits the home has exchanged roles with the parent and so there is a healthier interchange than if the teacher insists on maintaining a role which emphasises dominance and tends to obscure the fundamental role of the parent, without which all our classroom activities will be rendered almost totally ineffective. Usually, however, teachers themselves have not the time to focus attention on the child who may not be reaching potential. Indeed, unless an otherwise bright child shows inexplicable specific learning delays he is rarely a cause for concern in our present crowded classrooms. For instance, in the writer's own clinical experience it is rare to see a child referred because of problems of comprehension without the explicit or implicit assumption that he or she has a low level of intelligence. Yet teachers will commonly describe children who learn well from reading as 'slow readers' because they cannot read aloud and are slow to learn auditorily. At one time many such children, referred for hearing test, would have been discharged from the clinic as having normal hearing, although *no* test of auditory comprehension had been used. At one time the orthoptic department in our own hospital saw a number of patients with reading problems though, of course, most of these children had no defect of visual acuity. We all forget from time to time that most learning in the classroom demands an integration of sensory functions. Even though the acuity of the senses may be normal, integrative skills may be impaired. Integration depends not only on maturation and learning but also on the state of the physical integrative systems of the brain.

Reading

To illustrate this point, let us consider the problem of reading. The teaching of reading usually begins with the child looking at a group of visual symbols while listening to a teacher. Quite soon after this he is expected to look at symbols, listen to his teacher and immediately repeat what he has heard in order to develop the association skills. The child with problems of auditory memory or discrimination has already begun to fail. The child with problems of visual attention may continue to succeed in this limited sphere if he has good auditory memory. (To a considerable extent, 'look and say' reading places the onus on auditory memory in the early stages.) The extension of the child's developing skill to new and unfamiliar organizations of the same basic symbolic material tends to prove increasingly difficult in the two instances described above and so we are already faced with two possible sources of error which will cause loss of confidence and therefore failure. Once we recognise that learning to read involves an audio-visuo-vocal function it becomes evident that children can have excellent audio-vocal and audio-visual function, perhaps in certain cases even excellent visuo-vocal function and yet find audio-visuo-vocal function an intolerable problem. Sometime such failures stem from difficulties of attention (see below) and can possibly be helped by special tutoring. It is important to remember that the audio- and visuo-discriminatory processes have different time bases. With a permanent visual stimulus the eye can take time to focus, to extract figure from ground and to have as it were, a number of shots at external and internal scan. The auditory discrimination is essentially fleeting and hence two time-based regulatory systems need a specific skill in coordination which will not preclude utterance. Yet how often have we seen even the best reader stammer or stumble against a background of auditory distraction? What then of the child who, throughout his developing years, has perhaps not even advanced to a level of audio-visual parity in terms of attention or inter-sensory function? Other children have fundamental associative disorders or short-term memory problems which, while permitting silent reading, preclude reading aloud. During a period of responsibility for teacher training it was not uncommon for the writer to hear surprise expressed if a child performed better at reading comprehension than at reading aloud. Even now the term 'a beautiful reader' is only applied to the ability to read aloud, yet this is a skill which a minority of adults use. Have we, perhaps, got our emphasis wrong? Even if we have not, can we control the distractions which inhibit the development of those integrative skills demanded by reading? Even in silent reading we are sometimes faced with children who suffer from unusual problems of eye-control and hence of visual track. Some children can track down but not across the page. Some can read from right to left but not from left to right. (The writer once had a patient who could not read from left to right without immediately retracking the same line from right to left. Before this was detected the child was unsuccessfully attempting to match his auditory patterns to a confused agglomeration of visual symbols. Specialized therapy in which the visual stimuli disappeared as soon as the eye had tracked across them from left to right led to considerable improvement.)

Mathematics

From Piagetian studies we are aware of the stages of conceptual maturation and there is increased emphasis on learning concepts. This may pose problems for children who are expected to arrive at mathematical concepts from a study of actual objects or processes. For certain parents (and hence for their children) the notion of mathematical skill still hinges on enumeration or perhaps a parrot knowledge of number bonds. This, of course, ignores the whole basis of the creation of mathematical concepts by experience. Sometimes, indeed, such parents will regard these methods of education as 'just playing about with sand, water and scales'. There are some intelligent children who lack the kind of visual memory that such activities demand and hence are impaired in the development of the relevant mathematical concepts. Yet, at a linguistic (i.e. auditory) level, they have no problems of mathematical conceptualization. Such children will obviously need more time to develop the visual concepts, though the experienced teacher may well decide that if the child can manage problem-solving at an auditory level or even (as many do) at a symbolic (i.e. numeral) level this skill should be encouraged to develop first before returning, should this prove necessary, to practical experience as a foundation for the visual conceptualization.

Language and Learning

If we consider the significance of language in learning we may draw the threads of research into a clearer pattern. Kirk and Lyle, examining different populations at different times both showed that the subnormal child from the poor or culturally deprived home tends to gain more from additional educational facilities than does

c

the child from a home which offers a stimulating environment. We come close to the key to early learning if we look once more at Hebb's Theory of Intelligence and remember his emphasis on the interaction of 'Intelligence A' and environment. This key lies in the development of language skills. Language, spoken or written, is the meeting ground of minds, the basis for interchange of experience, information and emotion. A most interesting comment on the value and function of language is the emphasis made by Bernstein on its vulnerability and its modification by social factors. Language is a form of nourishment, lack of it will produce effects similar to any other form of under-nourishment, including impaired ability to absorb nourishment. Factors detrimental to language development, even if only temporary, initiate a cycle of inability to absorb. This results in reduced intellectual development which in turn prevents the continued development of skills already present, affects social skill and so holds up social experience and acquisition of information.

While considering development and learning we must remember that the emotional aspects of life are also to a considerable extent a function of learning and maturation. M. M. Lewis, discussing orectic development, described it as 'the progressive organization of emotions, the emergence of personality, the growth of social life, the differentiation of aesthetic criteria and standards, and the establishment of ethical judgement and conduct'. Russian research has indicated that the development of language may have a regulatory effect on a child's emotional life. As the emotions are given names, the child comes to discriminate them more clearly, to be aware of relationships amongst them, to organize them into relatively stable attitudes or patterns and so in some measure to direct and control them. Above all, language development may well play an important part in stimulating and maintaining the motivation to undertake and persist in particular patterns of behaviour. In thinking of these aspects we remember that communication systems (and in particular spoken language) are inextricably involved in the growth of self-awareness. The child's acts and the expression of his emotions evoke verbal approval or disapproval from others. As a result he becomes more clearly aware of his behaviour and attitudes as set beside those of other people. He realizes that he can obtain cooperation and approval or provoke resistance and begins to appreciate that he is as much the object of the behaviour of others as they are of his.'

We recognise that the child prevented from telling us *that* he knows is seriously affected. The child who cannot tell us *what* he knows is even more seriously affected. If he cannot tell us he cannot check his own accuracy. He cannot correct misconceptions, he cannot experiment with hypotheses on a fantasy level. Language is a means of legitimate self-display, it is a form of intellectual preening. Just as preening has a vital function in birds, so intellectual preening is vital to the development of information store, information validation, information extrapolation, vital to cognitive function, and vital to learning.

Learning is a skill – in saying this I am stressing that classroom learning is an acquired function. We learn to learn. Without communication the growth of learning is stunted. Without language the application of learning is impeded, without spoken language the communication of the fact and content of learning, though not impossible, is incredibly difficult. Our main problem is to differentiate between cognitive and verbal skills. Modification of either will of course lead to greater or less modification of both; we must be scrupulously careful to avoid the conclusion that impaired communication skill invariably springs from, or is an infallible sign of lack of intelligence. The problem is exacerbated by the fact that the majority of intelligence tests equate the two, and that as the tests are designed and presented linguistically, language failure is too easily mis-diagnosed. The child with any language modification is in serious difficulties on that basis alone. To compound this by adding an erroneous classification of intellectual impairment is an undeniable tragedy. Not only does it cut the child off from the specialized therapy which he needs so badly but it may well even cut him off from the education or general experience upon which his therapy and his developing language skills must necessarily build.

CONCLUSIONS

We have described reasoning as the application of the cognitive processes to past experience in order to make judgements about present or future problems; since it is obvious that language plays a very considerable part in reasoning, our role as diagnosticians, therapists and teachers is surely to ensure that the cognitive processes are given full reign so that past experience will, in fact, be applicable to future living. In other words, unless we have good knowledge of the type and extent of past experience we are in danger of attempting to build on extremely dubious foundations. How does the child develop his experience store? What is the basis of perceptual function, how does this lead to cognitive processes and how are we to encourage the display which has already been mentioned as vital to learning?

As teachers we recognise that we must optimise the child's own prejudgement of success by striving to increase confidence. We set out to convince the child *that* he knows, *that* he can succeed, so that he will put his knowledge to use. Because he knows, he is in a position of potential. Because we know he knows, he is in a position of reinforced potential. If he knows that we know he knows, he is in a position of strength. From this position he can move to a position of confirmation which further reinforces his self-regard, his confidence, his trust in us as supportive agents and his readiness to try again.

Owing to pressures on our psychological services neither the psychologists nor the teacher have been able to give complete and satisfactory service to children with learning problems. In fact, it is true to say that in a very large percentage of cases the needs of both children and teachers have not really been met. We need a clearer picture of the avenues of learning, of basic perceptual skills and in particular of specific assets and deficits. None of these, of course, will be given to us as a result of repeated requests for, or dependence on, Intelligence Quotients. The same situation will be equally true if we simply expect *scores* on the new Learning Aptitude scales. It simply is not good enough to show that a child scores. We need to know by what process he has scored and how such processes can be put to work in the classroom. In attempting to assess perceptual or cognitive potential we need to keep in mind the following facts about children with problems of learning. First of all each child is an individual with individual assets and deficits. These deficits are the result of an interaction of conditions and events and hence one would make a firm plea that we stop talking about '*the* backward', '*the* retarded' or '*the* slow learner'. The terms imply a homogeneity which does not exist. If it did the title of this contribution would be a different one and much of what has been written would be unnecessary. Children with learning problems may face some or all of the following conditions to a greater or lesser extent. These they master with variable success and so pose problems for the teacher which demand observational and descriptive skills of a high order if the optimum cooperation between teacher and psychologist is to develop.

A child may suffer from damaged sensory activity or inter-sensory organization, giving rise to impaired perceptual processes. This reduces experience and precludes or diminishes potential memory store. Reduced memory store results in low capacity to recall or encode and hence in reduced coding skills, which in turn leads to underdevelopment and hence to lack of further growth. In addition the child may have difficulties in discrimination and consequent problems of comparison between new stimuli and developed codes, where such exist. Diminished power of attention will lead to reduced expressive goals which will prevent full development of expressive skills. This is accompanied by modified attention at inter-sensory and sensory-motor level and results in reduced self-appraisal and the continuous self-awareness so necessary for further development.

All the factors described above may stem from psycho-physical or possibly neuro-motor conditions. Readers could, no doubt, produce a similar set of problems in motivational, social-emotional, intellectual or personality fields. All of these are intrinsic to learning and may well lead to learning delay or disorder. It is now more than twenty years since Magdalen Vernon stated that, 'We need tests of analytical skills by means of which we can identify strengths or weaknesses in the abilities to analyse constituent units or to organise them into the correct sequence or configuration. From this we could look for weaknesses or skills in generalising rules of combination and hence to re-synthesise or re-figure the constituent units in accordance with these generalised rules.' These comments, taken from her earlier book on *Reading Backwardness*, still apply equally well to all aspects of learning disorder.

From their own experience teachers will recall the child who for no apparent reason has given up and 'settled for failure', the class buffoon, so beautifully described by Morris; the child who decides that any answer is a sign of willingness and that willingness is a pathetic substitute for knowledge; the child who craves attention and has not the skills to earn it legitimately. He will also recognise the child who must be first, who cannot wait for a context to reveal itself but leaps into identify on the basis of the first familiar cue. Does the teacher recognise equally readily the child who finds visual stimuli an intolerable distraction, auditory stimuli a barrier to continuous thought, concentration on neuro-motor functions a bar to integration of other sensory inputs (most typically present in the child with minimal cerebral palsy or other neurological damage) or the one who needs prolongation or repetition of familiar situations or materials as a basis for security? Do we really know enough about the children in our care? How reliable is this knowledge? How is it obtained? What means of assessment are available to us? How objective are they? How are they recorded? Can we use these measures as a reliable and consistent means of objective measurement of progress? What size are our classes? How many classroom assistants are available? How many are needed? Would it be helpful if we did have someone to take over while we do concentrated individual work with children who require it? How are we to achieve the rigorous consistency and repetition some children need? Are the various mechanical or electronic audio-visual aids at present available to us a satisfactory substitute for the solid hard grind which is at present demanded of the teacher? How are we to achieve the minute specific gradations of progress which certain children seem to need? Would it be feasible to develop learning programmes which, while meeting individual needs, would prove sufficiently flexible to apply to other children without proving prohibitively expensive? Can we bridge the gap between laboratory research and classroom practice to the benefit of the children rather than the laboratory? How are we to persuade our educational administrators that without research no progress will be made while solving the practical and ethical problems that such research engenders?

Finally, in meeting the challenge posed by the child with problems of learning, can we make a clearer assessment of the reality of our ambitions for the children in our care? What are we really aiming for? Are we intent on joining the struggle because we enjoy a struggle? Do we see sufficiently clearly what we ourselves have to offer? What in fact, is the balance sheet of our individual assets – and liabilities? What in the end are we aiming for – the well-being of the child or our own gratification? One hopes that the answer is 'both' but that the latter will be based on a realistic appraisal of the former.

REFERENCES

B. Bernstein: *A socio-linguistic approach to Socialism* from *Directions of socio-linguistics*. Eds. J. Gumperz and D. Hymes. Holt, Rheinhart and Winston, N.Y., 1969.

D. O. Hebb: *The organisation of behaviour: a neuropsychological theory.* Wiley, New York: 1949.

S. A. Kirk: *The early education of the mentally retarded: an experimental study.* Urbana: University of Illinois Press, 1959.

M. M. Lewis: *Language and personality in deaf children.* N.F.E.R., Slough, 1968.

J. G. Lyle: The effect of an institution environment upon the verbal development of institutionalised children. (II) speech and language (III) the Brooklands Residential Family Unit. *J. Ment. Def. Res.,* **4**, 1–13, 14–23.

R. Morris: *The quality of learning.* Methuen, 1951.

J. Tizard and S. C. Grad: *The mentally handicapped and their families: a social survey.* Oxford University Press, 1961.

M. D. Vernon: *Backwardness in reading: a study of its nature and origin.* Cambridge University Press, 1957.

P. E. Vernon: *Intelligence and cultural environment.* Methuen, 1969.

S. Wiseman: *Education and environment.* Manchester University Press, 1964.

3

Some Aspects of Psychological Assessment

FROM ABOUT the last quarter of the nineteenth century the concern of psychologists was to demonstrate that psychology was a science rather than just a branch of philosophy. The vigour with which this aim was pursued may have suggested an almost neurotic preoccupation, and many papers increasingly sprinkled with jargon appeared. However, the work done by psychologists, particularly the results achieved in a variety of fields of human endeavour, has justified their claim and psychology is now accepted as a science. One of the tasks of a scientist is to quantify the variables with which he is concerned. For example, a physicist may measure the physical dimensions, the electrical resistance, and the heat capacity of a piece of metal. The metal can then be described in terms of its properties and predictions can be made as to its behaviour in certain circumstances; these properties and predictions can be applied to all other pieces of similar metal. The psychologist, however, who is concerned with human behaviour and who wishes to measure certain psychological variables has a much more difficult task, and his predictions are far less certain than those of other scientists, because the highly complex nature of human beings is due to many interacting factors. His measuring devices need much refining and modifying because he obtains different results from different people. Thus he may only be able to say that 'out of a population of x individuals y of them did so-and-so and therefore on a statistical basis I shall expect ....'; or, 'On Monday at 11 a.m. the individual A did so-and-so'. Compared with the traditional scientist the psychologist must be much less precise in his prediction about any individual. (It is worth noting, however, that the nuclear scientist is in the same position for he cannot predict that any particular atom of fissile material will split, he can only say that in a particular period of time a certain proportion will change.) Non-psychologists must therefore always be aware that when a psychologist makes a statement about the 'magnitude' of some psychological variable then he may be talking about an average value (of a large number of people) or that there are qualifications always to be borne in mind if it is about an individual.

So far as teachers are concerned the psychological variables which interest them most are those which help, or impede, learning. In particular they like to know how 'intelligent' a child is. A teacher usually makes a reasonable comparison of one child's ability with that of others and sees him as 'average' or 'below average' or 'above average' for the group. He does this both empirically and subjectively; the child learns more quickly or more slowly than the others, or he behaves 'sensibly' or 'foolishly' compared with the others. However, the teacher is frequently aware of the fact that the child learns one sort of material well and another badly, or he talks like an 'intelligent' child but makes no school progress and so we must speculate as to the cause of this lack of progress. One of the difficulties in discussing intelligence tests lies in the fact that there are many definitions of intelligence, but if we are to be concerned here with tests perhaps we might refer to the somewhat cynical definition occasionally used that 'intelligence is what the intelligence tests measure' – after all a piece of wood is said to have a length of, say, 50 cm because it is as long as 50 spaces on a special measuring stick.

We may see later that we have been misusing the word intelligence because it does not have the same meaning to all persons, not even to all psychologists. Part of the trouble lies in the fact that it may be used technically when attempts are made to define it, as for example:

Burt: An innate general cognitive ability, an inborn, allround intellectual ability.

Binet: To judge well to understand well, and to reason well.

Thurstone: The capacity to make impulses focal at their early unfinished stage of formation.

Terman: An individual is intelligent in proportion as he is able to carry out abstract thinking.

Thorndike: The capacity for association or connection forming.

Knight: The general factor which underlines all our thinking and comprises the power to discover relevant relations and the power to reduce relevant correlates.

Or it may be used in everyday speech, such as 'he made an intelligent use of his hammer'.

It will also be necessary to refer briefly to various suggestions, for example, that intelligence is innate or is a product of the environment, that the I.Q. is immutable or not. All these points are relevant when we consider tests as measuring sticks of 'intelligence' especially when we are not too sure what we are measuring!

In early attempts to assess intelligence (or 'ability' as it was called in England) workers measured certain physiological variables which were thought to correlate with mental ability. Thus, skulls were measured (and, in particular, some people thought that the size and location of 'bumps' were significant), or the ability to distinguish between various sensory stimuli was measured. Francis Galton, cousin of Charles Darwin, devised many such sensory and motor tests and was particularly interested in thresholds, the minimum stimulus perceived. Galton, himself a member of a family well known for the number of exceptionally talented persons it contained, believed that mental ability was inherited and this point of view has been widely accepted, and still is, by many psychologists and teachers as well as by the less-specialised man in the street. However, many people have been convinced that environment plays a major part in determining ability and this number is increasing. Cattell in America, using some of Galton's techniques and other forms of 'mental test', a phrase first used by him, suggested that such tests should be used to examine children; but it was Binet, a psychologist, and Inspector of Schools in Paris, who is generally thought of as the innovator of the modern type of individual intelligence test. (It was also Binet who introduced the word 'intelligence' in this connection.) Binet's problem was to select from Parisian schools those children whose ability was too poor to profit from normal school teaching. He devised a number of varied questions which seemed to him to assess different aspects of mental ability and gave these to large numbers of children. Since he wished his test to be independent of school-acquired information his questions were drawn more from everyday life, taxing in effect common sense, and he finally produced a single intelligence scale which he published with Simon in 1905. With his revised test in 1911 Binet introduced the concept of 'Mental Age', though many psychologists will now contest that this is a concept. Broadly speaking, if a child was able to answer correctly the items which Binet had established were answerable by the average eight-year-old then he said that child had a Mental Age of 8. Similarly, if he answered questions applicable to the average ten-year-old then he had a Mental Age of 10 and so on. Thus, Binet and Simon were able to say that a child's Mental Age was so many years in advance of or below his actual age, and if the retardation was large enough then this might be adequate for his removal from normal class. However, it is clear that two years' retardation in a child of six is more serious than two years' retardation in a child of twelve and in 1916 when Terman developed the revised form of the Binet-Simon tests he introduced the idea of the Intelligence Quotient, the I.Q.

I.Q. was then defined as the ratio $\dfrac{\text{Mental Age}}{\text{Chronological Age}} \times 100$

For practical purposes it was found that although intelligence (not I.Q.) increases throughout childhood, this increase slows down and finally there is no noticeable growth in intelligence after the age of about sixteen in the average person. Thus when calculating I.Q. by the M.A./C.A. ratio for persons over the age of sixteen, the chronological age is always taken as sixteen. If this were not done then it would be found that a person of 32 would have an I.Q. of about half what it was when he left school! Since Terman and many others believed intelligence to be predetermined by heredity, it followed that an individual's I.Q. must remain constant throughout life. In the Binet type of scale a question is considered to be appropriate to an age group if it is passed by half the children in that age group and failed by half, and a number of such items, say six, is then assigned to a particular age. Thus in the present form of the Binet test, known as the Stanford-Binet Intelligence Scale, to pass the items assigned to the eighth year, a child must:

(1) define eight words from a given list of words;
(2) answer five out of six questions relating to a one paragraph story which is read to him;
(3) explain what is silly about three out of four foolish statements;
(4) explain in what way three out of four pairs of objects are both similar and dissimilar;
(5) answer four out of six general comprehension questions which are mainly socially loaded in content;
(6) name the days of the week and answer two out of three questions relating to them.

If he passes all of these items but none of those assigned to nine and ten years or beyond, then he is said to have an M.A. of 8. If he passes them all and half of the items assigned to year nine he is said to have an M.A. of 8 years 6 months. In general the 'parts of a year' of M.A. which he obtains in the various items assigned to years subsequent to his basal M.A. (in this case 8) are added to that basal M.A. It might reasonably be thought that a child whose M.A. of 9 years is made up by a basal M.A. of 8 years +6 months from year 9, +2 months from each of years 10, 11, 12, is intellectually different from the child whose M.A. of 9 is obtained by passing all the items in year 9 and none beyond that. Hence the bald statement that two children of the same age have the same I.Q. on the same test, may hide a good deal of variation.

Since the test is devised in the manner described, by assigning questions to various age groups according to the percentage who pass them, it follows that the distribution of I.Q.'s in the various age groups must be the same, and although this is clearly an artefact of the test it has been used to support the theory that I.Q.'s are constant. But it merely shows that average I.Q.'s are constant for groups. Retesting of individuals also revealed a high degree of constancy and errors were thought to be due to errors in measurement. However, there appears to be ample evidence from numerous investigations, especially since about 1940, that an individual's I.Q. is not by any means immutable.

Reference has already been made to the way in which I.Q. figures may hide certain intellectual variabilities between individuals, and we all know of the person who is 'hopeless at mathematics', or languages, for example, and yet is competent in other work. In other words we are aware that individuals appear to have specific abilities and disabilities and this immediately engages us in discussion as to whether general intelligence is an integration of several mental abilities, or whether it is a factor which is common to these various abilities. If we set a traditional type of history examination, we can see that we are testing other things as well as history. Thus, we are testing the ability of the candidate to read and to understand the questions, we are testing his ability to remember, his ability to marshal and organise the results of his recall and his ability to write it all down. Thus there may be a correlation between for example, reading ability and examination score. Spearman examined the intercorrelations between the scores obtained by groups of individuals on various tests and by means of a statistical analysis showed that 'all branches of intellectual activity have in common one fundamental function (or group of functions) whereas the remaining or specific elements seem in every case to be different from that in all the others'. In other words there was a general factor 'g' common to all the abilities being measured, together with certain specific factors 's' peculiar to each ability. This has been called the Two Factor Theory of intelligence. 'g' was regarded as a sort of mental energy, possibly like a head of steam capable of operating various engines (s). Spearman did not call 'g' 'general intelligence' but many other people have done so. Although the Two Factor Theory has not had universal acceptance it has profoundly affected the thinking of educational psychologists and has led to the development of tests which purport to be 'highly saturated' with 'g', while others have been developed to assess specific abilities.

Wechsler has developed a form of test which appears quite different from the Binet type and which assumes intelligence to be the summation of different sorts of ability. The Wechsler Intelligence Scale for Children (W.I.S.C.) is widely used by psychologists when examining children between the ages of about 8 and about 16. (It may technically be given to children as young as 5 but many psychologists would refrain from this because of certain anomalies.) Wechsler makes no reference to the term Mental Age but goes directly to I.Q. The W.I.S.C. may be thought to have advantages over the Binet because it examines and reports on both verbal and non-verbal ability. Thus it consists of two Scales, Verbal and Performance. Each Scale consists of six 'sub-tests' of which five are normally given. Each sub-test consists of a number of questions or items. The actual score which a child obtains on a sub-test is converted into a 'scaled score' according to his age. Thus if a child between 9 years and 9 years 3 months obtains a score of 23 on the Vocabulary sub-test, then this is worth a Scaled Score of 8, whilst the same score by a child of 15 years is worth a Scaled Score of only 3; 23 by a child of 8 is worth 10, and 12 by a child of 7. Thus at the end of the examination a child has five sub-test Scaled Scores in the Verbal Scale and five in the Performance Scale. By a statistical device the total of these scores may then be converted into a Verbal I.Q. and a Performance I.Q. and the overall total may be converted to a Full Scale I.Q. However, let us consider two different children of the same age who obtain Scaled Scores on the Verbal Scale of the W.I.S.C. as follows:

Name of sub-test	Bill's Score	Ben's Score
Information	10	15
Comprehension	13	10
Similarities	15	9
Vocabulary	15	12
Digit Span	8	15
Total:	61	61

The total scaled score of 61 corresponds to a Verbal I.Q. of 114 so that both Bill and Ben have the same Verbal I.Q. However, the 'profile' of Bill's sub-test scores is quite different from Ben's and since the various sub-tests are assessing different aspects of ability it is reasonable to suppose that there may be considerable functional differences between the two boys. Thus from a superficial examination of those scores we might guess that Ben has a better 'general knowledge' than Bill but since his scores on Comprehension and Similarities are lower he might be poorer at applying logic to certain types of question. On the other hand he appears to be far better than Bill at concentrating for a short time on a rote memory task and Bill might be seen by his teacher as distractible. These are hypothetical of course and the psychologist who gave the test would have noted other factors which might well negate our very mechanical (and not very accurate) survey of the figures. However, the two sets of figures do serve to show that identical I.Q.'s cover several intellectual variations even in children of the same age.

Again, let us consider the case where one child has a Verbal I.Q. of 118 and a Performance I.Q. of 132, whilst another has a Verbal I.Q. of 133 and a Performance I.Q. of 115. They will both have a Full Scale I.Q. of 127 yet one would expect them to be very different in their ability both in school and outside. Nor will this necessarily appear as simply one being better at words than the other who is better at practical tasks. It could be and probably would be, far more complicated, and it could well be the case that the child with the lower Verbal I.Q. and higher Performance I.Q. is the better at formal academic work. However, these are highly technical and clinical points and do not concern us here. In fact, with such widely disparate Verbal and Performance I.Q.'s there is little justification in quoting a Full Scale I.Q. When Verbal and Performance I.Q.'s are about the same value, then they and the Full Scale I.Q. are usually not much different from the I.Q. obtained from the Stanford-Binet test for children between about 8 and about 15.

The tests which have been described so far, the Binet and the Wechsler Intelligence Scale for Children, are individual tests calling for special skills in administration, scoring and interpretation, and the W.I.S.C. is available only to specially qualified professional psychologists (though the Binet is also available to certain medical practitioners) and they take an hour or more to administer. It will be clear from what has been written that the psychologist will not be content to 'give an I.Q.' when he has completed his assessment. Indeed he may not give an I.Q. at all, indicating only in general terms the level of the child's ability. He will, however, expect to qualify his assessment by reference to specific failures and successes, aptitudes, attitudes and interests, so that in a psychologist's report on a child one will normally expect to find a considerable amount of detail qualifying any indication of intellectual level.

There are other individually administered tests mostly restricted in use to psychologists and some of them devised to be given to children with certain handicaps. The results may be comparable to those on the Binet or W.I.S.C. but if I.Q.'s are quoted then the name of the test should also be given. One should note too that a child with spasticity in both arms and a W.I.S.C. Verbal I.Q. of 100 has very different capabilities from those of a deaf child with a Performance I.Q. of 100, and both are different in capability from a non-handicapped child with an I.Q. of 100.

In addition to individually administered tests there are group tests, which as the name implies may be given to a whole class at a time. They are usually (if not always) pencil and paper tests, and there are verbal group tests and non-verbal group tests. In the former the child is faced with a large number of written problems which generally speaking become more difficult as he progresses through the test. The test consists of several sections, each with its own type of question, though in some tests the types are mixed. The questions are generally designed to test the ability to discover relevant relations or to educe correlates. The problem is usually answered by underlining, crossing out, or by marking as in a check list. The following are typical of the sort of questions which may be asked:-

Opposites Hot is the opposite of (winter, damp, cold, nasty)
Light is the opposite of (night, day, dark, cloudy)

Happy is the opposite of (miserable, jolly, painful, ugly)

Analogies Sun is to dry as rain is to (sky, puddle, wet, cold)

Knife is to cut as pen is to (ink, write, ruler, paper)

Perfume is to nose as colour is to (paint, brush, ear, eye)

Series Underline the two numbers which come next:

1   5   9   13   (16   17   19   21   23)

3   7   12   18   (19   25   33   40)

Mixed sentences Arrange the sentence in your mind and underline the correct word in the bracket: Berries the hedges eat to good all growing in are (true, false).

Although the ability to answer questions may depend to some extent on information which has been taught at school, most of them can be tackled independently. Inevitably, however well the test has been standardised on well-chosen samples of the general school population, cultural background will affect the children's ability to answer some of the questions. Thus, in the examples quoted the word 'perfume' is probably used more and therefore better known in certain areas than in others. The lack of knowledge of the word will not prevent a child from answering the question because the other words in the question may give him the clue, but the child knowing the word probably gets there more quickly. It seems impossible to develop 'culture free' tests.

Children who can read usually enjoy these tests. The score which a child makes is compared with those made by other children of his age when the test was being standardised. The comparison shows whether a child does better or worse than most, and by a statistical technique we can attach a figure giving an indication of how he compares – this figure is the I.Q. In some tests it is called a 'Standard Score'. Most group tests give a Standard Score or an I.Q. without proceeding through a measurement of Mental Age. It will be immediately clear that the use of these tests is restricted since a non-reader will obtain no score, which is silly, since there are several reasons why a child may not be able to read besides being of low intelligence. Therefore a different form of test has been developed:

The Non-Verbal Group Test.

In this type of test the form of logic required to answer the items is said to be similar to that needed in the verbal test, but the problems are expressed without words, using instead a series of diagrams. Instructions are given orally so that no reading is required. The following examples might be found in such a test: Underline the *two* which are like the examples:

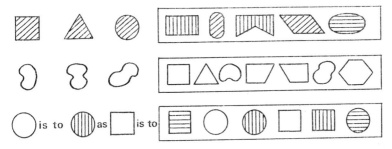

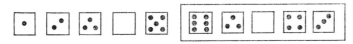

Underline the one which fills the missing space:

These tests are scored in the same way as the verbal group tests and from them non-verbal I.Q.'s may be obtained; scores which enable us to compare one child with others of the same age. It would seem then that since these tests can be dealt with by the non-reader we now have a method of assessing the ability of any child. However, there are children with particular difficulty in the field of visuo-spatial perception who may be unable to deal adequately with these tests. Such children may well have experienced undue difficulty when learning to read by 'look and say' methods and so score badly both on verbal group tests because they are poor readers, and on non-verbal tests because of their perceptual difficulties. Children with perceptual difficulties such as this do not necessarily (or indeed usually) have any defect in vision but they may fail to appreciate distance or they may be less able than most to discriminate between different shapes. This may be constitutional or it may be due to lack of the appropriate early experience. This illustrates one of the risks of using these tests alone as diagnostic of *overall* ability, since a low score may indicate rather a *specific* disability. It is true that this is of considerable educational significance and failure to realise its existence may mean that the child fails to receive the sort of special help that he needs.

D

Emphasis has been placed on the importance of paying attention to remarks which should appear in a psychologist's report qualifying his assessment of a child's intellectual level. The psychologist may have observed the child in the classroom or in a child guidance clinic playroom and report on his observations, but the bulk of his remarks will probably derive from his observation of the child in the controlled test situation and from his interpretation of test pattern. No such detailed observations can be made in a group test situation, so that a group test can give us little more information than the bare I.Q. which, as has been indicated, is of limited value. Nevertheless it may be useful to know just how I.Q.'s are distributed among the population so that the relevance of a particular figure may be discerned.

It is said that intelligence is distributed 'normally' in the population at large. It might appear obvious that it would not be distributed 'abnormally' but the word 'normal' here is used in a statistical, technical sense. Thus the height of adult males (or females, or fir trees) is distributed normally, that is to say most are around average and as we move farther from the average, above or below, so we find fewer individuals. If we draw a graph of the number of men against their heights we should obtain a 'normal distribution curve': so that while a large number are between 5 ft. 6 in. and 5 ft.

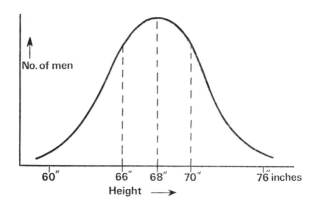

10 in. tall, very few are shorter than 5 ft. and very few are taller than 6 ft. 4 in. The form of this curve enables predictions to be made as to the numbers of men deviating in height by more than so many inches from the average.

It is said then that intelligence is 'normally' distributed in this way and the results of giving the Binet test to large numbers of children do form this curve. It is worth pointing out in this connection that the manner in which the Binet test is constructed makes a normal distribution almost inevitable. This does not invalidate the hypothesis of the normal distribution of I.Q. but it does not necessarily confirm it. The Binet test and others are constructed so that the 'standard deviation' is about 15 points of I.Q. The 'standard deviation' is a statistical measure of deviation from the average and when it is applied to the normal distribution curve it tells us the percentage of cases in certain categories. Thus in the case of I.Q.'s, given that the standard deviation is 15, we know that about 68% have I.Q.'s between 85 and 115 (100−15 and 100+15) and that about $2\frac{1}{2}\%$ have I.Q.'s below 70 or above 130 (100−2 × 15 and 100+2−15). When a new test is constructed it is 'standardised'. This means that it is given to a large group of subjects (who constitute a cross-section of the population) and then if necessary modified so that it gives a mean I.Q. of 100 and a standard deviation of 15. This obviously gives scope for cynics and sceptics but we need to remember that most of our measuring devices, be they pint pots, tape measures or tyre-pressure gauges, are standardised by being compared ultimately with some arbitrary measure. When we use a metre rule to measure a length we obtain a result which is accurate to the nearest 0·5 mm. for example, according to the quality of the rule and our eyesight; when we use an intelligence test there are similar caveats, some of which have been indicated in this chapter.

Reference has been made to the arguments as to whether intelligence is inherited or not. To some extent attitude to this is governed by the current social/philosophical thinking of the day and place, and it may therefore be difficult to achieve the desired degree of objectivity in studying this problem. The beliefs of Galton and Terman have already been mentioned, and among English psychologists Burt was probably the foremost in pressing the point of view that general ability is innate, and he probably became accustomed to seeing himself quoted slightly out of context as writing 'capacity must limit content: it is impossible for a pint jug to hold more than a pint of milk, and equally impossible for a child's attainments to rise higher than his educable capacity permits'. He goes on to explain that there will be many exceptions to this, but on the whole it is the view which he appears to support. On the other hand the American psychologist Watson wrote '. . . we no longer believe in inherited capacities . . . give me a dozen healthy infants . . . and I'll guarantee to train any one of them to become any type of specialist I might select, doctor, lawyer, artist . . . or thief'. It is these extreme points of view which have probably led to the over use, under use, and certainly misuse, of intelligence tests. It has also probably led to some of the confusion which exists as to the use of the word 'intelligence'. So far as psychologists are concerned it is likely that the most acceptable concept of intelligence is that expressed by the American psychologist Hebb, who sees the word intelligence as having two meanings, (1) an innate potential for development which is associated with the quality of the brain and an innate 'ability' to develop a good neurological system, while the other (2) is the actual level of the functioning of that brain and neural system, the day-to-day expression of ability. Hebb termed (1) Intelligence A and (2) Intelligence B. P. E. Vernon has proposed the term Intelligence C, which is the result obtained on intelligence tests. Intelligence A cannot be assessed and presumably never will be, but it is the object of test compilers that Intelligence C shall approximate as far as possible to B. Certainly Intelligence C, and for that matter B, can be shown to be modified by environmental conditions. No test is 'culture free' so that every test favours individuals with one sort of background and experience and disfavours others. For this and other reasons a child's I.Q. can be modified by the sort of experience he has, and by his total background.

Much in this chapter may seem to indicate that intelligence tests have little or nothing to commend them, and that their results are suspect. However, that is not the intention. It is the hope however, that teachers in particular should realise the limitations of tests and also their positive usefulness, especially where test performances can be qualified, as is often the case with individually given tests. A well-constructed intelligence test *does* give an indication of the way in which a child has developed an organisation for dealing with certain methods of approach, of making judgements, of reasoning and understanding, and to that extent it is a better single predictor of educational success that most other types of test. This is operationally true whether or not the test is an approximate indicator of Intelligence B. If it is found that a child performs substantially better on the test than his teacher would have expected him to, then it is more likely that the teacher has underestimated his ability than that the test has overestimated it. Possible reasons for the lower estimate by the teacher are that the child has an unsuspected specific disability, that he is emotionally upset or that there is some other factor leading to his underfunctioning. Such a child should receive a more detailed investigation; probably carried out in the first place by an educational psychologist in the hope that such individual examination may lead to recommendations as to how the child may be helped to realise his potential more fully. Even if this were the only result of giving a group test it would probably be thought worthwhile.

In the use of group tests teachers probably cannot do better than to choose from those provided by the National Foundation for Educational Research. The N.F.E.R. produces a range of verbal and non-verbal group tests which are suitable for children between the ages of about 8 and 15. It is unlikely that meaningful results can be obtained from a class of children much younger than 8, however good the tests may be. All the manuals of instructions accompanying the tests emphasise the importance of adhering exactly to the printed instructions and it really is important that this is done, both in the use of the oral instructions and, where necessary, in timing of the tests.

REFERENCES

C. Burt: *The backward child*. University of London Press, 1937.
D. O. Hebb: *Organisation of behaviour*. Wiley, 1949.
J. MeV. Hunt: *Intelligence and experience*. Ronald Press.
P. E. Vernon: Psychology of intelligence and g., *Bulletin of Brit. Psych. Soc.* No. 26.

4

Help in Reading

HELP IS NEEDED

AT ALL times the teaching of reading is a complex task, if the children concerned find learning difficult then the task is obviously greater. It has been recognised for some time that no one medium or method of teaching provides a solution for all children, therefore a large selection of books suggesting different approaches and presenting well-tried ideas is essential if teachers are to receive the help they so often need. In this present age all aspects of reading come under the microscopic eye of newspapers, journals, conferences, radio and television. Compared with the beginning of the century the public are much more aware of the problems and it is inevitable that some facets are so magnified and artificially isolated from the whole situation that often unsupported statements become too easily accepted. Statistics concerning the number of children who are non-functional readers vary, the true figure probably is not known.

Whatever the methods of teaching, however good the schools, there will always be some children who find reading difficult. Complete failures are not proportionately numerous but many children are inadequate readers when they leave school and consequently find reading laborious and uninteresting for the rest of their lives. Other children master the mechanics of reading at a fairly early age, but this skill is not developed during primary school days and their reading does not measure up to potential ability. All these children require help. No matter what the cause of reading failure, no matter how large or small the gap between anticipated levels and actual level achieved, the situation cannot be remedied by the child alone. The most vital indispensable reading aid is an understanding adult *with time* and particularly, in a remedial programme, the personal approach undoubtedly produces better results.

We all realise that the quality of teaching and teachers varies to an enormous degree. Those who are concerned with helping children with reading difficulties are often called remedial teachers. Some do this particular work by choice and have taken advanced courses to provide them with the extra knowledge they feel the work requires. Others are guided into the work because their part-time appointment fits in with the remedial reading time-table. Some less able teachers believe that taking the 'backward class' makes fewer demands on their abilities. Consequently not all remedial teachers are enthusiastic about the task assigned to them. Not all head teachers appreciate the value and importance of the work devoted remedial teachers are trying to accomplish with often difficult and uncooperative children. The keynote to success with such children is constancy and security, yet as soon as there is a staff shortage it is the remedial teacher who so frequently is requested to fill the gap. Valuable time with their own groups is lost and continuity disrupted. The importance placed on the teacher as well as the quality of teaching contributes to the progress made. Those who struggle daily with slow-learning children realise only too well that motivation is the key to success. Without strong motivation all methods fail; it is only the patient, concerned teacher who is able to establish a relationship with a child in order to discover and pursue every avenue of interest.

HELP – FOR WHAT?

We read in order to obtain information or pleasure. It is a way of communicating with people of other times and places. The normal sequence of development is listening followed by talking and then, a few years later, reading and writing. Reading involves the decoding of visual symbols into meaningful language and the encoding of language into visual symbols. Since reading and language cannot be separated the development of both depend on the exchange and interaction of ideas expressed by people. It is sad, therefore, to reflect that so many teachers feel guilty about talking to and with children. The poor reader often needs specific help with language, some children need training in careful listening and following simple instruction. Listening to children, deliberately trying to converse with them, all this is most important. It can take a long time to forge a link between teacher and child, but until this is established those who have become accustomed to a background of constant failure and ensuing rejection will never acquire the confidence and security needed for learning to take place.

Invariably it is assumed that reading is a once and for all happening. Some teachers believe that when a certain reading level has been achieved children can be left to go their own way, to use the library without help and to follow no structured programme. Some children are capable of developing their own reading with very little guidance but others are quite lost. Time is often wasted by children searching for information; when some relevant passage is found they then proceed to copy this wholesale into a self-made book. In this way 'beautiful' books can be produced without any true understanding of the contents. Training in reading and interpretation is required, the word 'training' being used quite deliberately in this context. Reading together within spoken language must be considered as a continuing process: and one that need never cease. Some of the major steps in this development are worth noting, especially since children with learning difficulties often have weaknesses in one particular area. In the early stages the following factors are relevant.

1. Physiological: health, hearing and sight.
2. Emotional maturity.
3. Intellectual maturity.
4. Language development:
    (a) being able to interpret pictures;
    (b) being able to relate a sequence of events;
    (c) being able to repeat the theme of a story or poem.
5. Visual discrimination:
    (a) identifying colours;
    (b) identifying similar and different shapes (two and three dimensional);
    (c) identifying similar and different letters.
6. Auditory discrimination:
    (a) identifying similar and different sounds;
    (b) identifying and producing rhyming words;
    (c) repeating sound patterns.
7. Left to right direction:
    (a) making left to right lines in confined space;
    (b) following picture story, placing pictures in sequence.

The next stage in development concerns the word recognition skills. These can be learnt by:

(a) the acquisition of a sight vocabulary;
(b) the ability to deduce some words from contextual clues;
(c) the ability to break down words into sound units;
(d) the ability to blend sounds.

Once children can read fluently then certain study skills need to be taught and practised; these include:

1. being able to select the main idea from a passage;
2. arranging related ideas in sequence;
3. summarising a book or part of a book;
4. using a dictionary, index and table of content;
5. using reference books;
6. making things from directions;
7. reading maps;
8. reading and acting on instructions.

All these fields of study skills develop comprehension and help children to evaluate and retain the material they have read.

Speed reading is an advanced skill which to date has not received a great deal of attention in schools. Perhaps the need to read quickly is a modern one, certainly some people have foreseen this need and recently courses on rapid reading have been established and machinery to train this ability is just becoming available. Those who have learning difficulties will feel added pressure if the question of speed is pursued. Even when mechanical proficiency is established, 'reading' can be a very slow process and simple exercises to increase the speed can be an advantage. Slow reading can impair and impede comprehension.

HELP – BUT WHY?

It will be found on investigation that children experience varying degrees of difficulty in learning to read. Some children will have made no progress at all with any of the skills mentioned above, others will have progressed so far and cannot proceed further until particular weaknesses have been diagnosed and a definite structured attack made to repair the gaps. It is not intended to search deeply into the causes of reading difficulties. This has been done frequently. There is never one cause and never one clear solution, each child must be considered as an individual and it is quite wrong even to attempt to group them into categories. One must avoid spending so much time seeking the cause that none is left to effect the cure. It would be ridiculous to underestimate the need to build up a complete profile of each child. Teachers know that some causes cannot be rectified by them. These include, among others, insecure home background, long absences and ineffective teaching. Whilst the cause cannot be removed, the reading situation can be improved in the light of all circumstances discovered. Children too need to know why they are failing, wherever possible, and this can be explained to them in simple terms so that they can be involved in their rehabilitation. From the beginning it is senseless to make light of the situation, but it must be made clear that success is possible once a combined concentrated effort is made. Short goals are essential and obvious failures must be avoided. Reassurance should be continuous. Unfortunately any prolonged look at children with reading difficulties often reveals many weaknesses and seldom just a single one. It is better to concentrate on the strengths but these do not necessarily exist and a multi-sensorial approach often provides the only way to success.

HELP – BUT WHEN?

Learning difficulties are not always apparent in the infant school child. Here, even the variation in intellectual abilities is not so obvious to the teacher – precociousness can be misleading. The differences between the dull and the bright child become much more evident in the junior school. Whilst early diagnosis is welcome and infant school teachers must be trained to observe intelligently, the first two school years should be a period of growing and adjusting to a situation which is quite new in many aspects. At this stage it is very important to keep detailed records of each child as these can prove invaluable later on. Reading readiness is a hotbed for argument, no tests with English norms are available and teachers' intuition is relied on to give judgement. There is a great need for more information in this subject. Whilst some teachers assume that 'better too early than too late' is a good policy to follow, it would be far more satisfying if there was less guess work involved in estimating reading readiness.

Until recently, any attempts to help the child with reading difficulties have been postponed to a fairly late stage. Remedial teachers became part of the secondary scene twenty years ago. More recently though it has been realised that help in the primary school can be far more effective. When children move from the infants to the juniors (usually 7+) they move also into a period of group activity. Working or playing alone is no longer so satisfying, it is being with others and accepted by others which becomes all important. Group membership makes certain demands on all members if working together is to be successful and whilst every child has something to contribute, the inability to read can make some children very loathe to join in group activities. Poor reading is difficult to hide and children can be, and often are, totally ruthless to each other in such a situation. At the beginning of the junior school the child is starting to realise his own limitations and this is when a cry for help is observed. If this is not recognised, more serious disturbances may reveal themselves all too quickly.

HELP – BUT HOW?

To suggest that all children with learning difficulties should be separated from their peers until the difficulties have been overcome rather reflects an acceptance of streaming; this is not intended, but for a short time each day these children need individual help, often over a long period of time. It is not always possible for the class teacher to absorb this additional responsibility and the cooperation of an extra teacher is required. Sometimes this extra work is carried out within the classroom, other teachers prefer to take the children away from the main group into smaller, more intimate, surroundings. Unfortunately in the newer schools it is becoming increasingly impossible to find a small quiet area where the child and teacher can work together in comparative peace. Surely each school needs one room which can be especially set aside for the children who need extra security and a closer contact with the teacher. The stock room/staff room/medical room is entirely inadequate, thus some authorities have established special centres in no way connected with particular schools. This system is ideal for the remedial teachers since the children do the travelling. Just how effective the two approaches are would be extremely difficult to measure. Some children welcome the opportunity to remove themselves from the school environment, others tend to prefer the surroundings they know. Not all schools are given additional help, so that the class teacher has to attempt very individualised and specialised teaching within a large group of children of mixed ability.

This presents almost insurmountable problems and it is only the highly organised dedicated teacher, probably with an exceptional ability to programme varied work with tape recorder or language master, who can possibly hope to gain any ground at all with the child who is failing. Whilst it is agreed that children with learning difficulties must be given the opportunity to take part in as many of the class activities as possible, it is also important to provide the individual help they need. As in all school activity, a teacher with a deep understanding and strong interest is needed.

HELP – FOR WHOM?

Specialist teachers trained to help children with reading difficulties are not plentiful; those who do exist should be used to the very best advantage. Some children require more urgent help than others and yet who is to decide who has the greater need? Remedial groups in schools can easily become the dumping ground for children who do not fit in with the class situation, who require constant attention and supervision but who are not necessarily the children with the most severe learning difficulties. Remedial classes can also become the dumping ground for teachers!

Within the limits of our present knowledge the remedial teacher, in consultation with the head and staff, should decide which children need help. There will always be difficult decisions to make – whether to give twenty minutes to one child or ten minutes each to two, whether this child can survive in the classroom or benefit more from extraction. The choice must be made after reviewing reading levels, potential attainment, age, attitudes to learning and general behaviour. Flexibility is important, rigidity within groups and between teachers will never restore a child to a normal working day. Whilst large numbers of children in the lower ability groups find themselves in 'opportunity' classes, it is hoped that the more able child, not functioning to full potential, will also receive the help required. Many of these are missed unless a good screening programme is in operation. Such children appear to be working on a level with most of their age group, yet sometimes a much higher standard could be achieved.

HELP – BY WHICH METHOD?

We all agree that learning to read can be a most exciting experience, and on this experience depends the whole future pattern of learning, the whole approach to school and everyday life. Whilst television and other technical advances have eliminated some of the need for acquiring this skill, at the same time society is increasingly demanding more and more reading and at faster speeds. 'Go here', 'go there', 'fill in this form', 'buy this', 'don't buy that' – instant reading requiring instant response. It is not surprising that the teaching of reading receives so much attention from publishers, authors and innovators of ideas. New media, such as the initial teaching alphabet, widen the choice of a 'way in' but an initial decision concerning method has to be made before the medium to be used can be chosen. I.T.A. can be used with any method. Such issues as phonics versus 'Look and Say' will never disappear from the scene so long as teachers remain responsible for their own choice. Perhaps no argument exists, certainly many teachers have never accepted the premise that there was an either/or choice to be made, but for years have quietly selected a method best suited to the individual child, very frequently a mixture of everything available. However, children with reading difficulties have problems, and it may be because earlier training has been too biased towards a single approach that the difficulties have persisted. If children cannot retain whole words, then obviously a breakdown of words is strongly advised. Flash cards are used very extensively in the first stages of reading to teach a basic sight vocabulary. Usually the first words taught to children are those they will find in their first reading book. These are not necessarily the words naturally used in speech, so from the beginning the situation is contrived.

The first whole words taught should concern the child's interest and experience, otherwise motivation will never survive, and it may never begin. *Breakthrough to Literacy* by Mackay, Thompson and Schaub, is an authentic attempt to introduce interest words in the initial stages. The 130 core words which the children learn, by using, have been selected from children's writing. This scheme allows for each individual to add his own words and gradually build them up into his own basic folder. The basic principles of the 'Breakthrough' scheme can be adopted for any age. Many of us agree that getting the children to *use* words is the first essential step to real reading. If a whole word method is used the words themselves must be carefully selected. Where possible whole word teaching should also involve the use of another sense – touch. Labels, alphabet frieze, flash cards, can be made occasionally with three dimensions. Wooden or plastic letters mounted on card are ideal, so too are the newer flexible magnetic letters which have the added advantage of being movable. Education is fortunately progressive, but not all old ways should be discarded and forgotten. Children using sand trays to make letters and words are not often seen, yet for some this tracing in sand can help reinforce a weakness.

Children with reading difficulties may require phonic help. Whilst we all realise that our language is not regular, nevertheless some constant patterns do exist. Basic rules must be taught systematically and thoroughly, and opportunity to practise these rules should be given as often as time allows. The children will inevitably gain a great deal of confidence by discovering that they can master some new words by applying the rules. Eventually some children will find the irregular words interesting because no rules apply. The idea of 'rebels' often appeals tremendously, and sometimes these words are remembered more easily than the others. Generally speaking, an analytical approach to phonics is easier to introduce – it simply entails teaching sounds from known whole words. The synthetic approach is somewhat more artificial, since it involves teaching sounds in isolation and then making them into words. Whilst no research has ever proved one way superior to the other, the analytical approach is more interesting and natural. (In the field of reading much of the research has only proved that one teacher using one method is better than another teacher using another method.)

Here are some basic teaching guides for phonic work, first of all the consonant sounds

b	n	
d	p	
f	qu	x
h	r	y
j	s	z
k	t	
l	v	
m	w	

These are taught in groups together with some of the vowels. The order in which these are taught is not known to be important, but many teachers feel that some sounds are easier to learn than others. Permanent alphabet friezes firmly fixed to the classroom walls have been popular in the past for easy reference. If one word and one picture is constantly associated with a sound, there is a possibility that every word beginning with 'a' becomes 'apple' to the child. It is much better to have a movable alphabet frieze, each letter represented in this way:

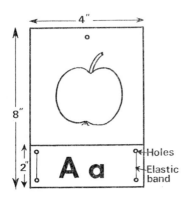

A row of drawing-pins with hooks placed at a low level will enable the children to hang up the frieze in the correct order, using a reference card until the order of letters has been learnt. As an additional activity a box of small pictures can be sorted and placed into the appropriate 'sound' box. A pocket on the bottom of each alphabet card is designed to store these pictures. It is made by placing a small piece of card (2 in. × 4 in.) flush with the bottom of the big card. Punch four holes as indicated and thread some narrow elastic through the holes and knot. This enables the pocket to stretch and will prevent the card tearing easily. With this game children will begin to realise that many words begin with the same sound.

Two consonant rules
1. 'c' has two sounds, k and s. If followed by a, o or u it says 'k'; if followed by i, y or e it says 's'.
2. 'g' has two sounds, ga and j. If followed by i, y or e it says 'j'.

Six vowel rules
1. Vowels can have long and short sounds.
2. If there is only one vowel in a word it usually has its short sound.
3. If there is only one vowel and it comes at the end of a word it usually has its long sound, me, no.
4. If there are two vowel sounds usually the first takes the long sound and the second is silent, e.g. *meat, pain.*

5. If there are two vowel sounds, one of which is a silent e, usually the first takes the long sound and the end e is silent, e.g. rose, gate.
6. If the only vowel in a word is followed by an r, the vowel is controlled by the r, e.g. fir, far, for.

Four consonant digraphs cannot be taken apart

ch
sh
wh
th

Twelve digraphs can be taken apart but are better taught as blends:

br	sl	st
tr	fl	spr
gr		
cr	cl	
fr	bl	
str		

Remember that not all children find phonics easy to master. Those who have poor auditory discrimination will respond more quickly to a visual and kinaesthetic approach. But many older children who are not reading have failed to understand the meaning of word attack, indeed they have not been shown any way of dealing with new words, or how known words are composed. Words can be satisfying and not terrifying. Oral games, taped lessons, board games, can all help to make the learning of these skills enjoyable.

HELP – WHICH BOOKS TO USE?

Immediately after the war, when the quality of reading in many of our schools was understandably very impoverished, books for older children with reading difficulties were almost non-existent. Now, nearly thirty reading schemes for slow learners are available, and if you consider also the thirty-five schemes designed for the initial teaching of reading at the infant level, the selection extends to over one thousand books. Even now the area of choice is not a constant one; indeed, at the present time it is extending too rapidly. Teachers are bemused and bewildered by all the books available. In the initial stages, Goodacre's survey (*Educational Review*, Nov. 1968) revealed that many schools are using more than the basic reading scheme. The other interesting feature of this survey was the seeming lack of knowledge about the range of materials available. Only seven of the thirty-five schemes were being used by more than ten per cent of the schools. No similar survey has been carried out among remedial teachers, but surely a different pattern would emerge. Teachers of children with reading difficulties use an extremely wide variety of books, they do not have to be purchased in large quantities for a whole school and obviously greater effort is made to meet the specific needs of individuals.

Unlike the infant reading schemes which have remained sadly unchanged over the past 25 years, schemes for older children have improved beyond recognition. Many of the early reading books designed for five-year-olds are dull and dreary beyond belief, and have no relevance at all to the child's own language and general interests. Indeed, some of the schemes for older children would make excellent 'starters'. Children who have failed to read at the expected time present problems concerning the interest level of books we place before them. This problem rises very sharply as the child grows older and moves into the secondary school stage. Oddly enough, the problem decreases after the children leave school. Adult illiterates who have usually 'volunteered' for reading instruction do not particularly worry about the reading matter provided the end result is achieved. Motivation exists, it does not necessarily have to be stimulated.

The actual choice of books is a personal one, no equivalnte *Which* publication exists for books. Reviews by different people can give most conflicting evidence and publishers' catalogues are inevitably biased. Selection of books should be made by the teacher, if possible after examining all the books available which meet a particular need. It is essential to study the following: (1) vocabulary control, (2) size of print, (3) introduction of new words, (4) illustration, (5) interest level, (6) how far the scheme develops, (7) introduction of phonic work (if any!) (8) contents of teacher's handbook. It is always advisable to purchase one set of books and use them with children. In the end this is the most reliable basis for judgement, but even children vary and we can all make mistakes. A brief description of the schemes available will be found useful and at least narrow the choice. All of us could produce a list of favourites but this would not serve any useful purpose. Publishers are accustomed to quoting interest age levels in their catalogues; these can be very misleading and seldom based on any acceptable criteria, the same applies to reading age levels. To describe a

E

series of books as suitable for children with reading ages of seven to nine years gives us very little valid information. The need for more accurate assessment of reading levels of books is acknowledged, but interest levels will never remain stable. These relate directly to the child's social maturity and this is not necessarily related closely to either chronological age or mental age. (See *Books for the Retarded Reader*, Hart and Richardson.)

In most cases children with reading difficulties have passed the infant stage before any real attempt is made to give special help. Because of this, basic reading schemes intended for five- and six-year-olds are not usually suitable. Some of the older, more established, schemes have an interest level more acceptable to the two-year-old. However, not all reading schemes must be dismissed in this way.

Many basic reading schemes are available, although it must always be remembered that children who have failed at the infant level in one particular scheme are much in need of something fresh when specialised help is available. Indeed, some children become very anti-books for a while, so it is as well to consider other ways of introducing a sight vocabulary and some of the basic phonic rules. Support materials can be used with books to provide practice and reinforcement.

HELP – THROUGH MACHINERY

The teaching of reading must take cognisance of modern educational approaches. In some subjects new techniques and new teaching aids have already proved to be of value. Until recently the teaching of reading took place almost entirely through the medium of books and blackboards, sandtrays and slates. Talking to a retired infant school mistress of eighty-three revealed that in at least one local school even books were not used to teach reading – no reading scheme was thought to be necessary but only the weekly purchase of a comic! This is not the picture now. Some children lack concentration and this characteristic persists well into the primary school. Variation in approach helps to maintain and extend interest. This is very much a visual world and books are not the only source of information and pleasure. Many poor readers are able to read the television advertisements, the projected word will often make an impact where the written word has failed. Audio-visual aids can be terribly expensive, only in exceptional circumstances can they be purchased to meet the needs of a few children. Sometimes it is possible to share the machinery with other schools and other teachers. This seems a sensible idea but it requires complicated organisation. Without a doubt all the audio-visual aids demand knowledge and enthusiasm from the teacher. It is difficult and extremely time-consuming to produce adequately programmed material, and at the present time the very little software available is often poor and expensive. Children with specific reading problems cannot usually make use of material originally written for the much wider 'average' market. Individual programmes are often required. It is hoped that more prepared material will be published in the near future. Meanwhile, many teachers produce and use excellent materials which help to counteract the weaknesses of the slow-learning child. No one machine is superior to all others, and teachers will vary in the priority they give to their purchases. Fortunately, once in the schools, machines can be used to support many facets of teaching. Film-strip projectors are already in general use in schools, but not necessarily incorporated into the reading and language programme. Some projectors do not require blackout, so small group or individual work does not interfere with other class activities. Suitable filmstrips are available from various publishers, some of which are coloured reproductions of outstanding children's books, such as *Winnie the Pooh,* and *Peter Rabbit.* These strips have no captions but they can encourage children to talk freely when adding their own commentary, and will often stimulate a desire to read the book. Other filmstrips tell a story through captions on each picture. Practically no published reading scheme has coloured filmstrips to support the books, yet these would be a most valuable addition to any reading programme.

Slide projectors can be used in a similar way; in actual fact filmstrips can be cut up and mounted into slides. This is an especially good idea where the smaller individual slide projector is available. Teachers are often able to make their own slides suited to the interests of individual children. Expeditions and events can be permanently recorded in this way. Even straight black and white photographs which are comparatively cheap to enlarge make stimulating reading books if mounted and captions added. The children's own plays, puppet plays and pets, can be used as the subjects for their own personal reading books with themselves depicted in the illustrations. Overhead projectors are very simple but most versatile machines, with no blackout being required. The 'software' (in this case acetate sheets known as 'foils') can be made by teachers, requiring no technical knowledge at all. By tracing or copying, a picture with captions can be produced quickly and easily using coloured felt pens or chinagraph crayons. By placing one foil on top of another children can see clearly how words are built up, and how they can be broken down. Once prepared, the foils may be indexed for future use or if not required again the picture washed off and the acetate reused.

Tape recorders, especially the cassette type, provide excellent reading aids at any level. They provide an almost unequalled medium for allowing children to listen carefully and respond. If a child does not hear or understand the first time the tape can so easily be rewound and played back. Prepared tapes are an expensive investment but some of them are good value since they do save the teacher endless hours of tedious work. Selection of suitable tapes can only be made by actually listening to them. Regional accents certainly present difficulties here, and too often the speed is not correct. The Language Master is basically a very simplified tape recorder. This small portable machine records and plays back a brief sentence. Cards are provided with a double tape on the bottom and space to write or draw on above. The teacher is able to make words or sentence cards incorporating pictures and text from reading books. By simple operations the child can record himself reading, hear himself read, listen to teacher read. This instant correction is most valuable. A prepared word study kit is available, also a set of Key Words to Literacy.

The *Talking Page* from Rank's is a portable, easily manipulated but expensive piece of machinery. Several reading programmes have been designed to go with this equipment. These incorporate a series of books and specially grooved records to go with each one. By means of a movable indicator even a small child is able to find the correct instruction for a particular page. The programmes are designed to be used without the help of a teacher though it is possible in parts for an incorrect response to pass by undetected and wrong learning can take place. Although several programmes other than the reading ones are designed to go with the *Talking Page*, use of this machine is restricted to the material which can be purchased. It is not possible for the teacher to design his own programmes. It has often been suggested to the writer that the Music Section makes admirable material for the child with poor auditory discrimination, listening skills are helped through a most enjoyable medium. There seems no doubt at all that the Talking Page is a great motivator, even with the most reluctant child.

Another machine which is new to Great Britain is the Synchrofax Audio Page. This synchronises the written and spoken word and since the material can be teacher-made it is adaptable to many situations. Apart from the machine, blank work sheets are purchased; these have a special writing paper on one side and a magnetic recording surface on the other instead of a conventional magnetic tape. Recording sheets are put on the Synchrofax machine which plays the four-minute recordings, the child can read or see drawings and pictures while listening to the spoken word. Each sheet allows four minutes of instruction and this is an adequate span for a child's concentration. It is far simpler than extracting four minutes of particular instruction from a conventional taped spool or cassette. The work sheets can be prepared to give practice in specific difficulties or designed to reinforce and consolidate actual reading. These sheets are easily stored for future use and are not expensive.

All these machines may serve to assist the teacher and the child. They all enable the child to work independently at his own rate. Responses can be checked almost immediately and errors corrected. The child with learning difficulties can enjoy working with machines because mistakes made are rectified without the knowledge of an adult and so a sense of failure is not so definite. Some will agree that the novelty of machinery soon disappears, but even so some learning will have occurred, and one more hurdle overcome.

HELP THROUGH READING GAMES

Teachers have always been innovators. Hours must have been expended on the devising and making of reading support material. Few reading games actually teach a previously unlearnt fact, but games provide a stimulating way of reinforcing certain rules and speeding word recognition. It is true to say that games can be quite unrelated to the true reading situation. Nevertheless, in the early stages and especially with children who are finding reading difficult, this playing with words and sounds can help enormously. Games can eliminate some of the more tiresome drill we associate with formal schooling. Games can encourage working together, appreciating rules; teachers must control the situation to some extent, so that each child is given a fair chance to win. Care must always be taken to ensure that reading games are not purely 'occupational.' It becomes obvious from some of the publishers' catalogues that the underlying purpose of games has not been appreciated. Often the rules are so complicated that a very high reading attainment is needed to interpret them. All games bought or made should fulfil the following requirements.

(1) Enjoyment: interest should be sustained for 10–15 minutes.
(2) Simplicity: the children who need games cannot absorb complicated rules, in any case these would detract from the underlying principles.
(3) Self-correction: this is not always easy to achieve but a game is much more valuable if a teacher can leave a group to play, knowing that mistakes are noticed immediately and correct responses rewarded.
(4) Suitable vocabulary content: games should provide extension to any reading programme, any sight words or phonics involved need to be directly related to the books the child is learning to read. If no one reading scheme is adhered to this is complicated. It is more sensible to use one of the word lists published, either Edwards and Gibbon's *Words your Children Use* or Burroughs' *Study of the Vocabulary of Young Children*, or, if a more restricted list is required, the core vocabulary from *Breakthrough to Literacy* or *Keyword to Literacy*.
(5) Ease of identification: reading games inevitably involve the use of many small pieces of card/wood/plastic. When found on the floor each piece requires an identification mark so that the children can replace it in the appropriate storage box. Coloured Sellotape is most useful for marking.
(6) Progression of difficulty: games must be well structured so that once the words or phonic rules are really known the children can progress to something more difficult.

Making reading games to meet the needs of various children at different stages can be a most tedious task. With the advent of teachers' centres, reading workshops can more easily be organised; here groups of teachers can meet together and share ideas as well as general resources. (See References for books with ideas that can be adapted.) Teacher-made games are always included in the permanent exhibition at the Centre for the Teaching of Reading, University of Reading. Games lend support to any reading programme but they should not be allowed to trespass too much on the time allocated to helping children to read. Surely all those experiencing reading difficulties will welcome the opportunity to 'play with words' but some children will never need this additional help.

S.R.A. Reading Laboratories cannot be rightfully included among books, machinery or games; nevertheless they are playing an important role in the modern trend of reading aids. None of the laboratories are designed especially for children with reading difficulties, but all of them can be used in this way. The material is extremely well graded and with the help of the teacher's manual it is fairly simple to pinpoint a child's particular weakness and there is clear indication how to direct each child into the section of the laboratory suited to his own needs. All children seem to enjoy the attractive presentation of each laboratory, even in large groups children can work at their own rate and vastly improve comprehension and speed of reading. Like all other aids, these laboratories can be misused and overused.

HELP FOR THE FUTURE

It is obvious that more and more reading aids and reading schemes will be developed over the ensuing years. Teachers and publishers must work in close cooperation to provide economically materials which will help solve some of the problems. Children with reading difficulties require individual help from specialist teachers. All teachers should be trained to observe reading development intelligently so that predictions of possible failure can be made and steps taken to rectify the weaknesses before the child becomes totally depressed by failure. This presupposes that all teachers are aware of the different stages of development in the normal child. Is this too much to expect? The reading teacher should be able to make a diagnostic assessment evolving a comprehensive profile of the child concerned. On this evidence a reading programme can be planned with the help of the class teacher and in the light of books, materials and time available. This also presupposes that a reading teacher or adviser is available to every school. Surely in the future this is what we should expect, teachers able to detect difficulties, and specialist teachers able to give well-informed help.

REFERENCES

P. Bell: *Basic teaching for slow learners.* Muller Educational Ltd, 1970.

G. E. R. Burroughs: *A study of the vocabulary of young children.* Oliver and Boyd, 1957.

J. Chall: *Learning to read – the great edbate.* McGraw-Hill, 1967.

M. Chazan: *Reading readiness.* University of Swansea, 1970.

M. M. Clark: *Reading difficulties in schools.* Penguin Educational, 1970.

J. Dean: *Reading, writing and talking.* A. C. Black Ltd., 1968.

R. P. A. Edwards and V. Gibbon: *Words your children use.* Burke, 1964.

E. Goodacre: *Reading in infant classes 1967. Teachers and their pupils' home background 1968.* National Foundation for Educational Research.

J. A. Hart and J. A. Richardson: *Books for the retarded reader.* Benn, 1971.

J. M. Hughes: *Aids to reading.* Evans, 1970.

S. Johnston: *Achieving reading success.* Cambridge Aids to Learning Ltd., 1969.

K. S. Lawson: *Children's reading.* University of Leeds, 1968.

S. McCullagh: *Handbook to Griffin Readers.* E. J. Arnold, 1964.

J. M. Morris: *Standards and progress in reading.* National Foundation for Reading Research, 1966.

D. Moyle: *Teaching of reading.* Ward Lock, 1968.

Reading Schemes for Primary Schools, Reading Schemes for Slow Learners. Reading Tests. School of Education, University of Reading.

V. Southgate, G. R. Roberts: *Reading – which approach?* University of London Press Ltd., 1970.

A. E. Tansley: *Reading and remedial reading.* Routledge, 1967.

B. Thompson, D. McKay and P. Schaub: *Breakthrough to Literacy.* Longmans, 1970.

M. D. Vernon: *Reading and its difficulties, a psychological study.* Cambridge University Press, 1971.

F. W. Warburton and V. Southgate: *I.T.A. and independent evaluation.* John Murray/W. & R. Chambers, 1969.

J. Webster: *Practical Reading.* Evans, 1965.

5

Mathematics for the Slow Learner

FOR THOSE responsible for the teaching of mathematics to the less well-endowed pupils in the secondary school there are two main problems: what should be taught and how to do it effectively. Unfortunately so much of what we do is traditional that very often we do not even ask these questions or perhaps we sense that there are no ready-made answers. The rapid changes in the teaching of mathematics, especially in primary schools, should be making teachers of older children who are slow at learning look afresh at the mathematics curriculum. Perhaps it is time to make a more realistic assessment of the needs of those who will never wish to take an external mathematics examination, feel the need to solve quadratic equations, use a slide rule, compute compound interest or use negative numbers. There are still too many teachers facing large classes of such wide ability that individual guidance is almost impossible. Mixed ability groups offer many advantages in terms of social development, but a pupil whose rate of learning is well below average also needs the help which comes from a careful diagnosis of problems, remedial exercises and a strong personal relationship with the teacher. Social workers, probation officers and employers who struggle with the problems of not only the illiterate but the innumerate would no doubt share this view.

The causes of poor attainment in school are complex and often mystifying. Usually many factors combine to give a low level of learning – physical, intellectual, emotional and social. The most common are slow maturation, poor attendance, environmental deprivation, emotional disturbance, and below average intelligence.

Initial testing of eleven-year-old entrants has revealed that among some there are particular weaknesses in language perception, memory and conceptual thinking. The most common disabilities are:

(a) difficulty in solving problems involving language,
(b) lack of ability to remember basic number facts or tables,
(c) confusion in the meaning of arithmetic signs $+ \times - \div$,
(d) no understanding of place value,
(e) little evidence of transfer,
(f) problems in counting, with little practical use made of the idea of grouping,
(g) uncertainty of the concept of fractions or area,
(h) an intuitive approach to a problem often resulting in improbable answers,
(i) confused ideas of methods of subtraction, multiplication, and division with impossible answers freely given, and
(j) poor work habits, frequent distraction, short periods of concentration and rapid fatigue.

These are the children we must set out to help by providing a realistic curriculum and methods which can minimise their handicaps to learning.

THE CURRICULUM

It is very unlikely that children with the difficulties listed above will go on to take competitive examinations in mathematics and so our aim must be to provide sufficient knowledge of the subject to give adequate social competence. What standard of arithmetic is needed by most adults in normal circumstances? There has not been much research to answer this question but three surveys, by Wilson in America, Moore and Thompson in England, all arrived at very similar conclusions:

(a) between 80% and 90% of all arithmetic was concerned with money,
(b) most problems were oral and calculated mentally,
(c) most problems concerned the addition of small sums of money,
(d) very little use was made of subtraction, multiplication and division,
(e) little over 5% of all calculations involved capacity or measuring,
(f) all need to tell the time, with occasional use of time-tables and
(g) some use of simple fractions, generally halves and quarters.

The syllabus for mathematics must therefore concentrate on

this minimum core of knowledge. The following basic aims are very similar to those suggested by a number of experienced teachers of slow-learning children.

1. Recognition of number values to 100.
2. Accuracy in counting to 100.
3. Addition and subtraction up to 100.
4. Grouping in twos, fives, tens and fiftys and hundreds.
5. Recognition of coins and their value.
6. Recognition of symbols for denoting money values.
7. Addition of money to £20.
8. Training in giving change by 'adding on'.
9. Practical measurement in yards, feet and inches, also metres, centimetres and millimetres, with rulers and tape measure.
10. Familiarity with finding weight, using different types of scales.
11. Experience with simple measurements of capacity using standard measures.
12. An understanding of the common mathematical terms used in everyday language.
13. Training in telling the time, including the use of the 24 hour system.
14. Simple budgeting.
15. Understanding pictograms and block graphs, etc.
16. Using a calendar and timetable.
17. Finding position using simple coordinates.
18. Using a simple scale to find distance.
19. Linking time and distance for travelling.
20. Talks on saving, insurance, hire purchase, rent and rates, bargains and the social uses of money

Some teachers may wish to break this syllabus into sections for different age groups. With many teachers taking the same children at different times there is the danger of a lack of continuity so that some system of recording what has been understood will greatly aid purposeful teaching.

Perhaps the hardest task of the inexperienced teacher of older slow-learning pupils is to appreciate how little they really understand, unless some familiarity with the writings of Piaget has led to trying some of his experiments; see, for example, Lawrence (1955), Lovell (1961) and Bunt.

Many ten- or eleven-year-olds will find difficulty in grasping the principle of conservation, e.g. that a pound of butter remains a pound of butter no matter what its shape, texture, colour or consistency. It is worthwhile for the teacher to repeat some of Piaget's experiments if only to prove the point to himself. Demonstrations in front of the class will arouse considerable interest, discussion, and argument, but the teacher must try to remain neutral, letting the individual child come to understand the concept in his own time. A simple exercise in conservation can be done with Plasticine and a pair of scales. A child balances two pieces of Plasticine on the scales, make sure to balance them each way by changing sides. The pieces are now accepted as the same weight. The question to be discussed is whether, if we change the shape we also change the weight. First stretch out one piece of Plasticine into a long sausage and test whether they are now the same weight. Compress one piece into a tight ball and reweigh. Now make a hole in the middle and compare again. Challenge the class – can you change the weight without adding or taking anything away? Even some eleven-year-olds will be astonished when the two pieces of Plasticine always balance. Those that are quite convinced it is some sort of trick are still at the pre-operational stage. Some who are half-convinced but not sure if the Plasticine is changed to sand will be uncertain. These pupils are at the intuitive stage. Only those who think the whole thing is obvious from the start are at the operational stage and will be sure that changes in the relationships of numbers in a group cannot alter the total. This can be verified by a simple game. Give each child ten counters and ask him to separate them into two piles, with eyes closed, keeping the counters hidden under each hand. Lift one hand and see how many are there and now guess how many under the other hand. Then play in pairs taking turns in guessing how many underneath partner's hand. Only when the child is right every time does he understand the concepts of conservation and reversibility for that quantity.

In the secondary school teaching by verbal explanation is still the commonest method. While communication can be made with brighter pupils, the use of lengthy explanations of method is seldom effective with pupils who are handicapped by an inadequate understanding of language. Berstein states (N.F.E.R., 1961):

> In arithmetic they may master mechanical operations involved in addition, subtraction and multiplication, provided they have

also mastered their tables, but they will have difficulty in division. However, verbal problems based upon these operations may confuse them. They will have great difficulty in ordering the verbal argument before applying the operations. They will have difficulty in generalising the operation to a wide range of contexts. Their conception of number will be restricted. Although such pupils may pass the primary stage without a great sense of unease, the discrepancy between what they are called upon to do and what they can do widens considerably at the secondary level. The central problem for such children is primarily that of learning how to learn, and to make educational experience happy and contented is not necessarily to solve the problems of learning.

The teacher trained in the formal uses of language continually complains of the limited linguistic skills and vocabulary of his pupils. Often the difficulty of sustaining or eliciting adequate communication appears insurmountable. It seems the child is speaking a different language. Berstein corroborates this belief and isolates it to a particular social class who feel little need for conceptualisation, but whose use of language is implicit, and whose communications are rather by non-verbal signals requiring a close relationship and empathy. The conditions of the normal classroom with an impersonal authoritarian method dependent upon formal language makes effective communication impossible and suggest that the individual teaching method in small groups, although fatiguing to the teacher, offers the best hopes for the close psychological relationship necessary to give a true learning situation. There are a large number of mathematical words in our normal vocabulary and the teacher of slow learners must not assume the child understands the mathematical concept implicit in the word, or the word for a concept which is understood. In many cases the word will have a restricted meaning or a limited association with some particular object or event. The teacher must be conscious of the need to introduce, expand and clarify the whole range of mathematical terms the children will need. Several lists of words have been prepared but once the teacher is aware of the children's inadequacy in understanding the mathematical vocabulary he will be on his guard against the difficult-worded question and the lengthy explanation involving the use of such words. In the small group situation the teacher will find it far easier to make his meaning clear and develop the children's vocabulary. (See reference list.)

CLASS ORGANISATION

Faced with the responsibility for developing mathematical language, arithmetical skills, adequate motivation, social competence, reasonable behaviour and individual help the teacher may well decide to find some less-demanding occupation. Certainly there will be little hope of success without the following:

(a) A maximum class size of twenty.
(b) A large selection of apparatus.
(c) Graded work-cards and text books.
(d) Diagnostic tests and individual records.
(e) Duplicating equipment.
(f) Wallcharts, handbooks, films and film strips.

The following suggestions may help the inexperienced teacher to decide how best to plan his teaching. Generally it is best to work on the '3 layer' principle.

(1) A foundation of work which is always available, graded and needing the minimum of explanation.
(2) An individual programme of graded work-cards or sheets for particular difficulties.
(3) A series of mathematical activities, set verbally or on cards.

Class teaching is used when a particular topic involves discussion and demonstration, for example, using a new piece of apparatus. Such a system leaves the teacher free to observe, question and help individual pupils, while allowing them the maximum opportunities for success. Behaviour problems usually arise where the task set is beyond the capability or understanding of the pupil. A sense of co-operation should be encouraged as some children will already be conditioned to be inconspicuously idle.

The emphasis given to each of these 'layers' will ultimately depend on the characteristics of the class and the personality of the teacher. There is no proof that any particular method is best and it is probable that, as in the teaching of reading to slow learners, the two factors most conducive to learning are the skill and enthusiasm of the teacher and a blend of methods to suit the situation.

Basic Work. The first task of the teacher of a class of pupils who have found little success in arithmetic is to restore lost confidence, to convince them that there are ways of finding answers without just trying to remember them or asking the teacher. This subordination of teaching to learning is helped by having available various types of apparatus, structural apparatus being of prime importance. In deciding which type to choose there are four main points to consider:

(1) Is colour helpful?
(2) Is size important? Small blocks can be difficult to handle, while large blocks take up a lot of space.
(3) Should the rods be marked? Marking tends to encourage one to one counting.
(4) Are there cards or books suitable for pupils who are weak at reading?

Some teachers may decide that more than one type of apparatus will be most useful, but one basic type should be established in the early stages to avoid confusion. Once the purpose of structural apparatus is understood, the children can confidently be left to discover the type they find most useful. Some directed practical activities given orally will help to establish the true meaning of the most common arithmetic operator. For instance, using rods the following methods could be used.

(1) Addition. Place the rods end to end. Measure with a ten rod. How many tens? How many units?
(2) Equality. Take a ten rod. Place two rods end to end beneath it to make the same length.
(3) Multiplication. Take 3 equal rods. Measure with a ten rod. How many tens? How many units?
(4) Subtraction. Take a ten rod. Find 2 rods equal to ten. Take one away. What is left?
(5) Difference. (a) Take one rod. Put a different rod underneath it. What do you need to make them equal?
(b) Take 2 rods. Place them end to end. Take 1 rod smaller than the 2 put together. Find what rods you need to make up the difference.
(6) Fractions. (a) Take a 6 rod. Find 2 equal rods to make 6. We say 3 is half of 6. The half can be written as $\frac{1}{2}$. The 1 stands for the whole length, the — stands for cut, split or shared, and the 2 shows how many equal rods.
(b) Take an 8 rod. Find 4 equal rods to make 8. We say 2 is a

quarter of 8. A quarter is written $\frac{1}{4}$. 1 for the whole length, the —
showing it is cut, shared or split and the 4 which shows how
many equal pieces (rods). What is a half of 8?

A well-graded series of exercises giving practice in writing the
number symbols and operation signs will be required. In making a
choice of books to be used it is important to take the low reading
age of the children into account so that one is not faced with a situation where the arithmetical difficulties have been minimised but
the language problem aggravated.

INDIVIDUAL WORK

It will soon become apparent that although we have commenced
an arithmetic programme which allows each child to explore the
world of number, there will be those who have specific difficulties
and need extra help or practice. Here is a challenge to the teacher's
ingenuity in providing individual activities and exercises which
will capture the child's interest. The very fact that the teacher is
supplying a special piece of work is often sufficient motivation in
itself if the work is at the right level. Here is a description of one of
the techniques used by the writer.

(a) On quarto-sized paper write out the exercise in pencil leaving
space for the pupil's name at the top. Have definite spaces or
empty squares for the answers and use the minimum of simple
language, the idea being an exercise the pupil can do on his own.

(b) Heat-copy using any one of the many types of machine available
to give a spirit stencil.

(c) Run off a number of copies and file in boxes or cabinet.

(d) File the 'master' copy.

The heat-copying stage is useful because it enables the teacher
to keep a master-copy and build up a file on each section of the
curriculum. Without this system the teacher would be unlikely to
have the time to prepare enough particular exercises, or would perhaps feel inhibited about changing a particular exercise because of
the work involved in preparing an individual work-card. The great
speed with which a copy can be prepared means the teacher can
provide exactly what is needed rapidly, give the pupil a sheet for
homework, and replace a sheet which is lost or spoilt easily. One
advantage over the traditional work-card is that the pupil has only

to write the answers on the question sheet in the spaces provided. This considerably increases the quantity of actual arithmetic done compared with a system requiring sums to be copied.

GROUP ACTIVITIES

The teacher of a class of less-endowed children will probably find that many of them will also have symptoms of maladjustment and immaturity. They tend to be self-centred and find difficulty in working with others as part of a team. Group work can help to develop self-discipline and good social habits, while providing opportunities for language development and concept growth. The best activities are those that arise out of the normal day's activities. It may be a birthday which prompts an activity connected with calendars, or the football results which begin a study of league tables. A boy may bring in an old gramophone, or a bicycle wheel, both of which can be used as a source of multiple mathematical activities. The teacher should also have a stock of stimulating material which can be brought out piece by piece at suitable intervals. Junior school teachers are well aware of the value of such mathematical project methods, but the teacher of a class of slow learners will need to be ready to give more direction in order to get a new project under way. When recording results, the children should be encouraged to try various methods of communicating their findings, using blocks or matchboxes to make graphs, cut-out paper, drawings, pictograms and models. The transition from the concrete to the abstract has to be patiently encouraged. The boy who is finding how much milk five cows have given may need to have five model cows and the model churns before reaching the abstraction of a set of figures. For very backward pupils R. H. Nicholls' experiments in programming Piaget-type activities would be worth studying by the teacher.

Activity lessons can be planned in three ways.

1. *Directed Activities*
   (a) Teacher chooses activity.
   (b) Demonstration and discussion.
   (c) Teacher isolates particular concepts involved and teaches the vocabulary needed to describe them.
   (d) Oral questioning with simple numbers involved.
   (e) Cyclostyled exercise.

F

2. *Partially-directed activity*

(a) Pupil or teacher promotes the activity.
(b) Teacher suggests approach.
(c) Discussion of material and apparatus needed.
(d) Teacher assists in recording results.

3. *Pupil-directed activity*

(a) Pupil chooses own activity with teacher's approval.
(b) Organises own material and apparatus.
(c) Records own results.

NUMBER. From the surveys carried out by Wilson, Moore and Thompson it is clear that, apart from specialist occupations, adults use number very little. House, bus and telephone numbers have to be read and understood in number form only. The sequence of number is needed when using rulers, tape measures, mileometers, as well as finding a particular house in a street. Accurate counting should be encouraged for checking quantities of goods, newspapers sold and as an aid to the shopkeepers' method of giving change. Multiplication is best begun as repeated addition with tables or ready reckoners as aids. The social use of fractions is limited and not common outside of halves and quarters. Boys may need to identify fractions giving sizes of bits and spanners but will not need the four rules of fractions. Much of the drill formerly associated with the learning of number after the initial concepts have been established using structural apparatus can also be carried out using decimal currency.

Hints on Teaching Number.

(1) Encourage an attitude of enquiry by asking questions, e.g. Does it matter which number comes first in that sum (addition/subtraction)? In number bonds, when one number gets bigger, does the other one always get smaller?

(2) When giving number exercises plan them so that the children have to discover something about the answers. e.g. What do you notice?

(a) $1 + 1 = \quad 1 + 2 = \quad 1 + 3 = \quad 1 + 4 = \dots$
(b) $0 + 0 = \quad 1 + 1 = \quad 2 + 2 = \quad 3 + 3 = \dots$
(c) $2 - 1 = \quad 3 - 1 = \quad 4 - 1 = \quad 5 - 1 = \dots$
(d) $3 + 5 = \quad 5 + 3 = \quad 3 + 6 = \quad 6 - 3 = \dots$

(e) $10 + 1 = 11$ (f) $10 + 1 =$ (g)   10   10   10
     $9 + 2 =$ $10 + 11 =$ $+ 11$ $+21$ $+31$
     $8 + 3 =$ $10 + 21 =$ —   —   —
     $7 + 4 =$ $10 + 31 =$ —   —   —
     $6 + ? = 11$ $10 + 41 =$
     $5 + 6 =$ $10 + 51 =$

The last exercise often shows a lack of understanding of place value. Much of this is due to the confusion caused by the same symbol having different meanings. Some children are helped by writing the previous exercise in two ways:

	1 ten $+$ 0	10	1 ten $+$ 0	$+10$	1 ten $+$ 0	10
add	1 ten $+$ 1	$+$ 11	2 tens $+$ 1	$+21$	3 tens $+$ 1	$+31$

A few lessons showing the use of an abacus will help to make the system of place values clearer. A diagrammatic form of the abacus can be used in remedial exercises.

(a) Write the number   —

Add 10   Add 20

(b) Which rod shows the tens? Add a ten bead. Write the new answer.

Certain games are useful in helping children to grasp place value. The teacher can produce a score board divided into hundreds tens and units in several ways.

(i) 3 compartments each holding only ten blocks. As the right-hand compartment is filled, one block is put into the middle compartment and the right-hand compartment is emptied.

(ii) Use the beads to show the score on a vertical abacus. Also useful is the board-type abacus using coloured tablets of L. G. Sealey which also parallels in concrete form the written lay-out of addition.

(iii) Simplified Billiards Scoring Frame with units at the top and tens along the bottom.

(iv) Counting Machines: a large variety of these are available.

Also bring the children's attention to the counting mechanisms on for example tape recorders, cyclometers.
(v) Games. Some may need modifying i.e. Bagatelle, by reducing numbers.

Subtraction. This entails separating a small group from a larger group. The difference may be visual or symbolised by counting and recording. The easiest method for slow learners is by counting on. This has to be taught as some children trying to find how many are needed to make 7 into 12 will start at 1 every time. When transferred to money the technique is known as the Italian or shopkeeper's method.

MONEY. The most essential part of the mathematics scheme is money. The elementary stages which may need re-teaching to slower older children are briefly:

(a) Coin recognition.
(b) Coins to symbols/symbols to coins.
(c) Addition, starting with lower value coins.
(d) Complementary addition to give change.
(e) Adding larger amounts by grouping.

The relevance of money as a symbol of value in the buying of articles is difficult to teach. The worth of objects is such a wide question that it cannot be confined to the narrow boundaries of mathematics. In this sense it is best included as part of a social study course.

Shopping exercises using money give some reality to our arithmetic, especially with self-service, making sure the dummy cartons are the same weight as that shown on the label and the totals are checked on leaving. Most shops will provide posters showing prices of goods but the best way is to price the goods in the shops. Ideally the slower children can run a real shop selling crisps, biscuits or apples. In most schools, however, the teacher will need to structure his money learning to give sufficient practice at each stage. Variations of simple shopping exercises would include 'Sales' catalogue ordering, paying fares, going out for a meal, simple budgeting and visiting the post office.

Hints on teaching Money
(1) Shoe-box lids, with exercises requiring the answers in coins, will stop the coins slipping on the floor. The exercise is written on the inside of the lid.

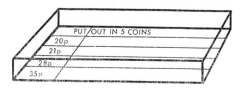

Variations

(a) Put out a fixed amount using different numbers of coins.
(b) Make up an amount to a fixed total.
(c) Pay for stamps or tickets with coins.
(2) Money dice. Money dominoes and various money games give extra practice.
(3) Cyclostyle bills for shopping.
(4) Let children make own shopping cards from old mail-order catalogues.
(5) Use bags from bank to collect coins for totalling.
(6) Make up sets of wage packets. Letter each packet and mark on the outside the coins that it should contain. This saves endless arguments about the total when some of the coins are on the floor. Have an answer slip for checking.
(7) Either cyclostyle or buy simple ready reckoners.
(8) Have a rota for collecting and checking dinner money.
(9) Dramatise social situations involving money, e.g. the wrong change, making a choice, buying a ticket.
(10) Make a survey of class savings, pocket money, starting wages.
(11) Show films on shopping, insurance, banking, hire purchase to promote discussion. Film strips on similar subjects are available.
(12) Consult the handbooks offered free by the National Savings Scheme.

MEASUREMENT AND TIME

Most work on measurement is best carried out in the school workshops. Graded exercises and practice may be needed in the classroom but should be as practical as possible. Brighter pupils can carry out simple surveying with chains or long tape measures to find missing measurements on diagrams of the school premises. Scale drawing and map work are possible if carefully planned to minimise possible complications. The measurement of area is most easily taught using plastic grids, and grids can also be used for simple work in coordinates. Most classes enjoy an exercise using a cyclostyled grid to find the 'treasure'. This also brings in some useful work on direction which leads to simple angles using a compass and circular protractors. If the teacher is aware of the limitations of his class in computation many interesting topics can be explored without great difficulty.

The true concept of time is only gained by experience and is very undeveloped even at the secondary stage. Ask a class to guess when a minute has passed and the estimates will be wildly out, but this fact can be used advantageously in discussing ways of telling the time, from sand egg-timers and candles to the newly-acquired wristwatch. The smaller intervals of time are easiest to learn. It is relatively easy to count seconds, but difficult to estimate hours. A clock on the classroom wall is essential but so are calendars. If we start with telling the time it is interesting to notice how small a part the numbers play when we look at a clock, and in fact many clocks now leave out the numbers. Check the wristwatches in the classroom, or look at the television clock. Clock time is given in three ways, verbally, as when we say twenty to four, and written, either as 3.40 p.m. or 15.40. The two most important are the verbal statement and the Continental written method. For the poor readers the verbal statement need never be written in full using words. A shorter way is to have a clock face marked with hours in one colour, minutes in another (see diagram). The hour hand should be the colour of the hour number, the minute hand coloured the same as the minute numbers. When the pointer is on the right the number is *past* the hour – when on the left it is *to* the hour. It is written as 25 past 3, ¼ past 4, 10 to 5 – in fact as it is said.

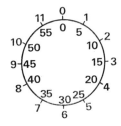

Then show the change to putting hours first, then the minutes and dropping the half and quarter past. 3.25, 4.15. Then comes the problem of minutes *to* the hour, which has to be changed to minutes past. Here the minutes marked on the edge of the clock face will help. 10 to 5 becomes 4.50.

Changing the dial to a 24-hour clock offers no further difficulties in writing down except the use of the nought as a space filler, e.g. 20.05 but it will take much time to get people to accustom themselves to converting 9 p.m. to 21.00 and many of our slow learners will find this difficult.

The most important work is in the first stage, and exercises should show a clock face with questions on what happens at the time shown, including some on the school timetable.

Children will generally find the use of second and minute timers much easier than telling the time and these should be used in the initial stages. Girls can make up cooking charts and boys time athletic activities while both can time various experiments in the classroom or radio and T.V. programmes.

We also need to record the days, months and years using the calendar, and keeping a record of birthdays, holidays, national and local events. All work written in school should be dated as part of this training and topics on time periodically given. Postmarks can be collected and show the time taken for delivery; lighting-up times and the hours of daylight can be graphed. Some training will be needed in calculating ages and writing dates of birth. Many boys, especially in towns and cities, will be vague about the seasons. For journeys we shall have to consider the relationship between time and distance and for those about to leave school we must study time and earnings.

THE LAST YEAR. The advantages of studying mathematics as part of a social study scheme are particularly obvious for pupils in the last year at school where they can become a natural part of many activities. Some knowledge of formal processes is essential, but only as a means of solving problems faced in everyday situations. The emphasis should be on making the situation realistic enough to motivate the pupil into finding a solution. This may also be linked with the responsibility for certain jobs involving numbers.

(a) Checking attendances.
(b) Keeping scores for games and checking equipment.
(c) Keeping a mileage record and calculating cost of running a school bus.

(d) Collecting house points and keeping a graph.
(e) Stocktaking.

In addition to such practical activities in school, pupils should be given projects which take them outside of school and involve them in experiences requiring numerical activities. Such visits are most useful educationally if done individually or in pairs.

(a) Buying stamps and posting letters.
(b) Buying a postal order.
(c) Accompanying secretary to bank money.
(d) Using a public telephone.

As the visits are extended, pupils will find a need for local maps and guides. The use of maps will lead to a need to understand grids, scales and compass bearings which can easily develop into exercises in navigation and planning road journeys including distance, time and cost problems.

School leavers should be trained in social service and, apart from shopping, other arithmetical activities may include laying a new lawn, buying seeds and plants, planning a tea-party for old people, and running a sale.

Many activities will involve pupils in problems which require simplification. When a method has been established by discussion using simple numbers the calculation of a total involving larger sums of money should proceed by realistic methods emphasising the value of estimation.

Ideally, methods and examples in mathematics would be related to the occupations likely to be followed by the unacademic pupils. However, little valid research has gone into making a detailed study of the mathematics required for everyday occupations. Teachers tend to set exercises based on imagination rather than fact. Anyone watching a carpenter at work on a building site quickly notices how little a ruler is used. A plumber can put in a complete central heating system without a single measurement, except by eye. The gardener spaces out his plants with a handy length of stick, not a tape measure.

The greatest use of mathematics will be in reckoning money. The casual worker may be earning three or four pounds a day shortly after leaving school and yet have little idea of the value of his money. Training in simple budgeting should be started early, with discussions on the rewards of saving and the dangers of over-spending and hire purchase. Classroom saving schemes for visits and outings may help to develop good habits, and records of individual savings can be recorded pictorially.

GAMES

Initially many pupils will play games without scoring, unable to face the difficulties of calculation. The teacher should modify such games by simpler methods of scoring, gradually increasing the numbers involved. Bagatelle boards or pin tables are always popular. Have a simple version with numbers up to 20, then introduce another with numbers to 50. Attach a small slate and chalk for scoring, or have a simple abacus or adding machine.

Dice games can be useful. A board divided into two parts, marked off in squares, and a cube marked with numbers and plus or minus signs is very popular. If the dice shows +2, then 2 counters go on to the squares, while −2 would mean taking 2 counters off. Variations can be introduced and a similar game can be made using decimal currency.

Shove-ha'penny is a game which can involve scoring, and a small skittle board is another test of skill which brings in counting. Billiards or snooker are valuable, especially if the proper scoring board is used. Darts, hoop-la, table tennis, cards including games like summit, all help to exercise pupils in computation as well as developing skill in popular recreations.

REFERENCES

P. Bell: *Basic teaching for slow learners*. Muller Educational Ltd., 1970.
E. Brideoake and I. D. Groves: *Arithmetic in action*. University of London Press, 1939.
L. N. A. Bunt: *The development of the ideas of number and quantity according to Piaget*. Wolters, Groningen, Djakarta, 1939.
W. E. Chambers: *I do, and I understand*. Nuffield Maths. Project, 1961.
E. M. Churchill: *Counting and Measuring*. Routledge and Kegan Paul, 1961.
L. W. Downes and D. Paling: *Teaching of arithmetic in Primary schools*. O.U.P., 1958.
D. H. Gale: *The teaching of number*. Hulton Press, 1963.
D. H. Gale: *Number language*. Hulton Press, 1964.
E. Lawrence: *Some aspects of Piaget's work*. National Froebel Foundation, 1955.

K. Lovell: *The growth of basic mathematical and scientific concepts in children.* University of London Press, 1968.

The teaching of mathematics in the primary school, The Mathematical Association.

N. A. Moore: *Arithmetic in the daily life of adults.* University of Birmingham, unpublished dissertation.

R. H. Nicholls: *Programming Piaget in practice.* Teaching Arithmetic, Vol. 1, No. 3, 1963.

W. W. Sawyer: *Designing and making.* Basil Blackwell, 1950.

L. G. W. Sealey: *The creative use of mathematics in the Junior school.* Basil Blackwell, 1961.

H. A. Shaw and F. E. Wright: *Discovering mathematics.* Edward Arnold, 1969–70, Bks. 1–6.

Thompson: *Special Education,* Vol. 51, autumn 1962.

A. A. Williams: *Arithmetic at the crossroads.* Spec. Education, Vol. 8, No. 4, 1963.

6

Art and Craft

THE CREATIVE use of materials is of paramount importance to the child, not only for personal development but also as a means of communication. The opportunity to experience and appreciate materials visually and tactually at first hand is a necessity for every child. Personal strengths and weaknesses, fears and delights, the world of fantasy as well as reality, may all be explored. This world of play leads to unlimited ways of personal expression. The experience individual children will gain in achieving the final result will vary due to many factors. For too long child art was judged by adult standards. The child should respond as a child in art and craft as in other subjects. Most of us owe our failure in this subject to being educated in it. We are reluctant to express ourselves visually because our standards are confused, and we resort to the folk arts of the twentieth century such as plastic kit building and embroidery from iron-on patterns, instead of the personal and creative craft forms practised by more primitive peoples. Art is individual and personal – it must be enjoyable and it must be worth doing.

The idea of developing the mind as well as the hands to work creatively seems to have emerged slowly. Education for leisure may well be the most important work we can do for coming generations and in the field of art and craft we have a major responsibility. The supermarket society has many advantages, but one of its weaknesses is that seller and buyer have little personal experience of the construction and quality of the manufactured articles they are selling and buying. There is little opportunity for either party to have first-hand knowledge of the materials from which the articles are made. This breaks a long tradition in the craftsman–customer relationship. Choice is often made because of the wrapping rather than on the qualities of the article itself.

Visual and tactile judgement are surely two of the greatest attributes inherited by children. We have deprived ourselves of the time to stand, look and touch. Let us help children to develop their powers of awareness and appreciation by encouraging them to explore materials visually and tactually in as many ways as possible.

COLOUR AND TEXTURE

The exploration of texture and pattern is an extension of the basic process of learning through tactile experience. The quality of texture is an important element of relaxation and helps to reduce tension.

The development of awareness to colour and texture and their relationships can be achieved in many ways. Colour has been regarded as a subjective concept too frequently. Green has been grass green, willow green, moss green, whereas it can be light or dark, rough or smooth, translucent or opaque, shiny or matt, large or small, thick or thin. Colour must be explored and played with because it has such an influence on all our lives. Collections of coloured scraps are fun, collections of all one colour are more of a challenge. Put together green papers: tissue, metallic, patterned; green fabrics: velvet, corduroy, hessian; green leaves, and arrange them into patterns or into pictures. Explore ways of applying green to a surface in different ways, for example, green ink on a porous surface, on glass, on corrugated paper, water-bound greens immiscible with oil-bound greens or green wax crayons. There are so many ways of exploring green, each with its own character and its own beauty. To some of us this is familiar, but to many here lies a world of personal discovery as exciting as any moon probe. Colour for its own sake can be enriching and satisfying.

Below are some ways of playing with colours that may lead to the discovery of many more.

1(a) Exploring colourants on a variety of surfaces

The surface may be paper, white or coloured. English, Swedish, Ingres and Mulberry papers come in superb and subtle colours but are expensive. Sheets of hardboard are initially expensive but can be used again and again by cutting the hardboard into a variety of sizes and painting with emulsion paint. Various colours should be used, for example white (common), matt black (unusual) and orange (difficult to deal with). When the work has been displayed and served its purpose the hardboard can be washed clean, recoated with emulsion and used again.

Painting on a plastic-coated surface offers further experiences.

If water-bound colours and markers are used the surface can usually be washed down and re-used, although red can sometimes stain. Sticky-backed plastic sheeting can be obtained in gold, silver and chrome as well as in simulated wood. Using pieces of hardboard, either painted or coated with plastic sheeting, gives children the opportunity to work on a larger scale than might otherwise be possible.

1(b) Mixed media

Powder colour can be used with a thickening agent such as cellulose paste, PVA binder or an alabaster filler. It can then be applied very thickly with a brush, stick or finger. Dry colour can be sprinkled on a surface already coated with cellulose paste. This surface may be left flat or folded to give mirror images.

Coloured or Indian ink may be dropped on a wet surface randomly, or the paper may be tilted to create runs. Alternatively, only small areas of the paper may be wetted out to control the colour spread.

Wax crayons or paraffin candles can be used as a resist. Draw with them on paper and then lightly brush over with water colour. This may also be done on a light cotton fabric. Wax crayons can be used to block out a printing screen.

Tissue paper can be torn or cut to the desired shape and then pressed on to cartridge paper already coated with cellulose paste or with PVA binder. The latter will give a translucent effect when dry, and will make an interesting lampshade if bent to a cylindrical or similar shape.

2. Rubbings

Positive or negative rubbings may be made on thin white paper. For negative rubbings work over the textured surface with a dark wax crayon. A large size wax crayon broken in half and used sideways is most convenient. Positive rubbings may be obtained by working with a white wax crayon or paraffin candle and then brushing over lightly with dark water colour paint.

Rubbings may be made from many natural materials, for example wood in its natural or machined state, especially if it has weathered, will produce interesting patterns, also feathers, leaves, pebbles may be used.

Man-made materials also offer many opportunities for taking rubbings. These include textured wallpaper and glass, textured fabrics, nets and laces, threads laid to a shape or random, expanded polystyrene, and building blocks.

Rubbings may be created by cutting shapes from paper or textured wallpaper and arranging them as a pattern or picture. Similarly string or thread may be pre-arranged and then rubbed. Rubbings may be taken of the impressions of paper clips, nuts, bolts, nails pressed into balsa wood, PVA binder or other adhesives trailed on to wood and then left to dry. The surface of a piece of hardboard, or a slab of plaster of Paris can be cut, scratched and textured to create a surface from which rubbings may be taken.

A collection of rubbings can be made and used to make a collage picture, by cutting out silhouette shapes and sticking them to a background. Similarly patterns may be made by repeating the same rubbing in a regular sequence.

3. Print making

There are two common methods of applying paint, or printing ink, to the object to be printed. One is by pressing the object into a saturated pad of colour, the other is by applying colour to the object from a roller.

The simplest way to make a printing pad is to tear up three or four pieces of newspaper and put them on top of each other on a non-porous surface. This non-porous surface may be a piece of glass, a tile or simply a plastic bag. The newspaper should then be saturated with paint and the object to be printed pressed into it. At the end of the printing session the pad can be thrown away.

When using a roller, a similar non-porous surface is needed on which to squeeze the printing ink, in order to coat the roller. Water-bound printing ink will serve on most occasions and it is easier to remove than oil-bound ink. Printing directly from a wooden or plastic surface is seldom successful as it is too hard. A newspaper should be put down first to act as a cushion.

Almost any article with a textured surface may be printed. Leaves and feathers are best inked then put on to a sheet of paper, covered with a piece of newspaper and finally rubbed or rolled down to make the print. Many objects may be inked and printed, such as buttons, matches, paper doilies, which may be printed individually, in rows, spirals as linear or radiating patterns.

Picture making by printing. This may be done in two basic ways, firstly by printing individual objects so that together they make a simple picture. A strip of strawboard 2 in. x 4 in. can be printed end on or edge on to produce a 2 in. or 4 in. line. From this matchstick men, railings, and explosions can be made. A more satisfying method of print picture making is to build up the complete picture on a piece of strawboard. Take a piece of strawboard 9 in. x 12 in. or larger and cut out from pieces of textured wallpaper or fabric the shapes required, for example, houses, trees, cars, figures, and stick them down with PVA binder to the strawboard. Additional pieces of paper, thread, or string, may then be applied to the basic silhouette shape to add detail. When the adhesive is dry ink over the strawboard and shapes completely with water-bound printing ink, black being probably the best colour to use and print on kitchen paper or newsprint. Such a block will give you at least a dozen prints, and smaller blocks can be made to print greetings cards. For further subject ideas see the section on picture making.

Multi-colour prints. Cut or tear out a silhouette shape, for example, a clown, from cartridge or other thickish paper. Ink this with a roller in the normal way. By drawing on the wet ink with a dry matchstick the ink will be removed and the subsequent print will show white lines. This is a paper print. Going back to the paper silhouette shape of the clown and cutting off his hat, head, shoes, then inking these all in different colours and reassembling them for printing, a multi-coloured print is obtained. A whole circus, zoo or farm could be made by a group of children using this method.

Print making offers endless possibilities for visual exploration, the element of surprise being not the least of these.

4. Surface texture

The application of pieces to a surface opens up new possibilities for visual and tactile experience. Various mosaic forms can be developed according to the materials available.

Paper mosaics These are the simplest to make and may be created from ready coloured paper, gummed or plain. English or Swedish coloured papers, Italian and French Ingres papers, Japanese Mulberry papers, colour magazines, old wallpaper are all suitable for this work. A sheet of cartridge paper (Imperial size) can also be coloured, using a large 1 or 2 in. paintbrush. Pin the paper with the narrow side to the top. Start by painting a band of red across the top, about an inch wide, then gradually introduce yellow to the brush, working bands across with more and more yellow until all the oranges to pure yellow have been used, then begin introducing blue and work through all the greens to pure blue. Introduce red again and work through the purple browns until red is reached again. This is a kind of rainbow which can be cut into strips parallel to the colour bands about $\frac{1}{4} - \frac{1}{2}$ in. wide, using a guillotine, so that a bundle of paper strips of every colour is obtained. These may then be cut into $\frac{1}{4}$ or $\frac{1}{2}$ in. squares as required.

Draw the outline of the picture on a piece of cartridge or sugar paper and paint in the area to be worked on with cellulose paste and apply the dry pieces. Leave narrow gaps between the pieces for the background to show through. White paper is the most common background, but coloured papers look more attractive. Working on some of the metallic finished sticky plastic sheeting, or oven foil, is unusual and worth doing. Areas of this applied to hardboard give groups of children an opportunity to work on a large scale.

General mosaic materials, These invariably need a firmer base than paper mosaics, $1\frac{1}{2}$ lb strawboard or hardboard being suitable. This should be coloured or coated as the paper base; black is very effective. The pieces should be applied to this base with PVA binder because although it appears milky in its liquid state the binder will dry transparent. Collections of seeds found in the garden and country give a wide choice of texture and colour and can be augmented with sawdust, sand, rice, pastas, cereals, iron filings, various bird and other pet foods. Begin by drawing the design on the base, paint in the area to be worked on with adhesive, then sprinkle on the material and press down under a piece of newspaper. Hold the baseboard on its edge and gently tap off the surplus, and then go on to the next area.

Abstract ideas are often as successful as naturalistic ones, for example, drawing out field patterns as they might appear from an aeroplane and then filling in with granules; painting spirals interlocking circles and other shapes directly with adhesive and sprinkling on granules. Using the same methods a much more sparkling effect may be obtained by using sweepings from a bead merchant, which are ideal for making decorations. Cylinders, small boxes, pyramids, mobiles may be made from coloured papers and decorated with sequins, beads and baubles. Screw tops from jars, the polystyrene trays from supermarkets may be filled with Plasticine or plaster of Paris and then seeds, collections of small stones, shells, buttons embedded into them to make decorative discs or rectangles.

PICTURE MAKING

Picture making covers a vast field, and includes many possible motivations and materials.

Young children seldom draw what they see, they draw what they think, and what they mean. They use varying forms of symbolism which we must respect, as adult standards are not their standards and a sympathetic understanding of this is necessary to appreciate and encourage children's work.

Children sometimes need to clarify their ideas before they begin painting. They may need to know, for example, which aspect of a subject might be stressed. Thus discussions of the mood of the picture, whether it is to be mysterious, gay, or exciting; the scale, which things are to be large or small, near or far; the media to be used are all helpful, may also be discussed.

The suggestions for paintings which follow may be worked by individuals or groups and may be used in many ways, such as finger painting, one of the finest ways of all for children to paint, or through brushes, pens, crayons, prints or relief modelling and carving.

Pictures

(1) Heads. These may be painted on paper about 12 in. high, or on paper cylinders to fit the child's head, or on strong paper bags. Examples to paint are clown, tramp, witch doctor, myself, TV or story character, animal faces.

(2) Decorative. Most of these may be made from boxes and card rather than simply painted, for example, nursery rhymes, Punch and Judy show, peep shows: toy theatres, games, model TV studio sets, record sleeves and book jackets.

(3) Imaginative, for example, haunted castle, pop music title, space station, Gulliver on his travels, tropical jungle, my street 100 years from now, the flood, the channel tunnel, the magic toyshop, weightlessness.

(4) Contrasts in light and shade. Many of these would be better painted on black or dark blue paper, for example, night train or flight, moonscape, circus, house on fire, burglar at a safe, potholing, the fairground, carol singers, the gunpowder plot, driving home on a wet night.

(5) Action pictures, for example, pop concert, the highwayman, car or motor-cycle race, earthquake, wreck and rescue, blast off, street accident, forest fire, hi-jack, emergency landing.

(5) Pictures from written description. Extracts from many books are suitable, which may all be illustrated by a strip story as typified in many children's comics. The value of these is only just beginning to be appreciated.

(7) Atmospheric pictures, for example, the storm, moonlit castle, count down, volcanic eruption, ambush, coming to school on a windy morning.

(8) Pictures based on personal experience, for example, going on holiday, ill in bed, my cat or dog, shopping, picnic, father decorating the house, my family at breakfast, mother bathing baby, going to visit my friend, going to the cinema.

(9) Men at work, for example, painters, roadmen, the dentist, traffic warden, the milkman, astronauts, builders, footballers, diver, commando.

(10) Topical events. Many public events, festivals and customs stir children's imaginations and interests, as well as topical events at home, for example, my sister's wedding, Hallowe'en, our house being painted, my new bicycle.

(11) Group work. Although many of the earlier suggestions are suitable for group work, the following lend themselves particularly to this type of activity. Friezes of the following topics may be made from painted cut-outs applied to backgrounds: on parade, a busy street, the farmyard, television studio, the zoo at feeding time, circus, airport, car rally. The following can be made on separate pieces and then assembled: the theatre; using circular pictures: the seasons, the creation, astrology; using applied pieces: row of buildings (see Fig. 1), a row of houses with gardens, pier, dockyard.

Fig. 1

(12) Work on film. The emulsion can be removed from old 35 mm film by rinsing it in neat household bleach. The clear film can then be textured and patterned with felt and fibre pens, coloured inks or

paint. The pieces of film should then be put in 35 mm. transparency mounts and projected in the normal fashion. Similarly, any clear non-inflammable material may be used. 8 or 16 mm ciné film may also be treated in the same way, although it is better to work down a continuous strip of film about three or four feet long, which can then be projected to produce a moving image.

THE EXPLORATION OF MATERIALS AND IDEAS IN THREE DIMENSIONS

Clay

Clay is probably the most elementary and satisfactory material children will ever handle. The tactile experience which clay gives cannot be replaced by any other substance. Its versatility is unbounded and offers endless creative possibilities. It comes in a number of colours, for example, 'Crank mixture' is oatmeal in colour and has a pleasant texture. It is ideal for making large objects, as it has a high grog content and is less likely to crack as it dries. 'St Thomas's Body' is more refined, smooth and again oatmeal in colour. Whitebodied clay is that normally used to make small objects which are coloured afterwards. Terracotta is a red clay which is very smooth to work with and is used for modelling. It is beyond the scope of this chapter to go into details on the actual technicalities of colouring and firing clay; there are excellent books already dealing with this.

Clay can be bought in hundredweights and will arrive in a plastic sack. If possible, it should be kept in a plastic dustbin on a duckboard with a little water underneath. A length of nylon fishing line with a toggle or ring tied to each end will make a clay cutter; small sticks make excellent modelling tools, especially if one end is cut to a point; modelling boards may be made from old plastic or lino tiles; detergent bottles make containers for liquids; old plastic bags can be collected for covering working surfaces, and for wrapping work which is to be kept damp. Clay needs to be kept soft enough to be manipulated by the children. If it becomes too leathery it can be sliced with a cutter, sprinkled with water and kneaded together again, this process being continued until the consistency is right.

Many of the ideas suggested for picture making might equally well be carried out in clay. Clay rolled out into sheets, cut into shapes and then modelled on in low relief, using characters from stories and the Bible, geographical or historical themes for these tiles or plaques. Tiles can be made quickly and evenly with a tile cutter. The tiles may be used for relief modelling individually or put together to make a large wall decoration.

Sheets of clay may be cut out to make clay boxes (slab pottery) or rolled round tubes of cardboard for cylindrical pots. The tube should be covered with wet paper first so that the clay can be slid off when it has hardened a little. All these shapes may be decorated by pressing into the soft surface articles such as paper clips, screw heads, straws, sawdust and iron filings.

Slabs of clay wrapped round smooth, gently tapering glass or plastic bottles make ideal foundations for modelling figures (bottle figures). A ball of clay is applied to the top to make the head and then further pieces applied to make the features, hands and hat. The bottle should be oiled or greased at the beginning so that the clay can be removed when it is leather hard. Sets of characters, chessmen, saints, Canterbury pilgrims, kings and queens may be made in this fashion.

Pinch pots or thumb pots may be made by squeezing a ball of clay into the shape of a small pot: thus here is the beginning of pot-making.

The best brushes for decorating clay are Japanese, which are made from animal hair.

Paper

Paper is another versatile material offering many creative opportunities. The traditional folk art ranges from the cut paper work found in China and Poland to the ritual paper funeral models from Hong Kong. One of the attractions of working with paper is that so few tools are required.

Simple shapes. Paper doilies are always a source of amazement and satisfaction to children. A circle or rectangle of paper is folded in half three times, the secret of success being to cut away more than is left. Many of the continental coloured papers look attractive when used for this purpose. Kaleidoscope-type decorations may be made by cutting three or four tissue paper circles about 4–6 in. in diameter, folding and cutting as doilies. These should be placed on top of each other with a pin through the centre so that they can be rotated to change the pattern. They may be stuck down with PVA binder which will safeguard their translucence when dry, or they may be sandwiched between two sheets of glass.

Polish cut paper work is a fine example of a traditional folk art still continued today. The small and sometimes multiple mirror images invite analysis and are an inspiration for further work. Such paper work is attractive, and may be used for its original purpose to decorate walls, doors, greetings cards, paper prints, or for needlecraft designs.

Another traditional method of working in cut paper is to apply one cut paper shape upon another. The silhouette shape of a bird may be cut from one coloured piece of paper, the wing shape from another colour and applied to the body, the flight feathers from yet another colour and applied to the wing.

Chinese cut paper work is quite different and equally beautiful – it is another source of inspiration for working with paper. Cartridge paper, English and continental coloured papers are suitable for cutting, and also oven foil if thicker paper is required.

Surface Texture. A piece of cartridge paper folded down its length, or in a more complex fashion, will give an edge to cut into (Fig. 2).

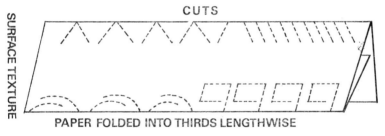

Fig. 2

These cuts can be folded and curled to produce surface texture and the paper then made up into a decorative cylinder. Similarly animal or fish shapes may be cut out and surface texture applied to these.

Sculpting with paper. Paper is suitable for making many things, such as simple shapes of flowers. The head is made from a circle with a slice cut out, edges of the slice are overlapped and stuck together to produce a shallow core, the stalk is made from a paper strip, the leaf from a small piece of paper folded lengthways, half the leaf cut out so that when the paper is unfolded the two halves appear as mirror images. All these shapes are stuck down on a paper background, singly or as a group effect.

A mask may be made by cutting an egg shape out of a piece of 8 in. by 6 in. cartridge paper. To turn the flat egg shape into a shallow cone to fit the face, a wedge-shaped slice is cut out from the bottom to the centre, overlapping and sticking together the edges of the slice. Eye holes and a mouth may be cut to suit the wearer. To make the nose a horizontal slot about an inch wide is made between the eyes. A piece of paper of the same width is pushed through from the back and pulled down to above the mouth, where it is stuck down. Ears, eyebrows, whiskers may be added and finally elastic can be attached to hold the mask round the wearer's head.

Moving paper constructions
These are much more exciting for children as they can also be used. The following examples lend themselves to painted or applied decoration.

Mobiles. These are always a source of interest and are simple to make if taken step by step. The construction of the individual components offers many opportunities to play with paper shapes. They may be made on a theme, for example the planets, ships, the circus, cartridge paper or aluminium foil being suitable for their construction. The centre bar can be made from wire coat hangers, strips of bamboo or any thin piece of wood (Fig. 3).

Glider. Nearly every child can make a folded paper glider, thus it is only a short step to making one out of thin card, with Plasticine or paper clips to weight the nose (Fig. 4). Following the construction, distance and endurance records can be made and measured.

Kites. Both square and diamond-shaped kites may be made from cartridge or coloured papers. They are ideal for decorating and may be waterproofed by coating with clear polish or model aeroplane dope (Fig. 5).

Pop-up books. These are best made within a folded piece of card and a number of them may be joined together to make a small book, perhaps interleafed with written work. Alternatively, single examples may be made and used as greetings cards.

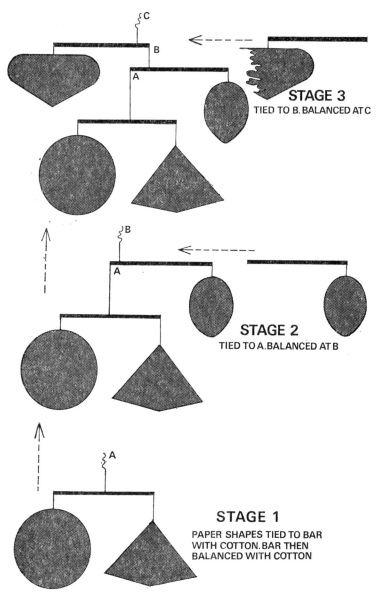

STAGE 3
TIED TO B. BALANCED AT C

STAGE 2
TIED TO A.BALANCED AT B

STAGE 1
PAPER SHAPES TIED TO BAR
WITH COTTON. BAR THEN
BALANCED WITH COTTON

Fig. 3

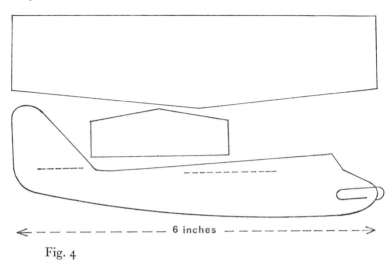

Fig. 4

Peep shows. The Victorian peep show offers an amusing way of making three-dimensional pictures. It can also be a very useful teaching aid. The front may be cut and painted to represent a theatre, or a hole of about $\frac{1}{2}$ in. diameter cut in it to make a true peep show.

Model theatre, TV sets. 12 in. x 24 in. peg board makes a suitable base for theatres and TV sets. The bases may be used singly or a number of them may be put together to make a sequence of sets. The set may be a simple one consisting of a series of flats one behind the other, or it may be a fully detailed model. The cut out card flats or models should have 6 in. or 8 in. lengths of 3/16 in. dowelling taped to the back with a small projection below the card to plug into the base. For a teaching aid model a scale of 2 ft.: 1 in. will match up with many plastic figures, animals and models.

CONSTRUCTIONS USING MIXED MATERIALS

Wood

Most timber yards will supply off-cuts of assorted timber free or at low costs. A tea chest is a suitable container for the timber and the following assortment of tools: a light Warrington or panel-pin hammer, a small hacksaw, pliers, rasps, rifflers, sandpaper, a drill,

[*Continued on p.108*]

KITE

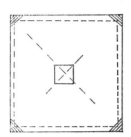

Cut cartridge or brown paper 20 in. square. Score a line $\frac{1}{2}$ in. along all sides. Cut off corners. Fold edge in and stick down. Stick 3-in. square in the centre to reinforce.

Cut four 2-in. squares from thin card. Cut each square in half diagonally. Place two triangles on top of each other and staple together through kite corners to make pockets for stiffeners.

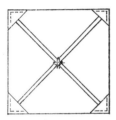

Cut two stiffeners 26 in. long. Slip these into the pockets at opposite corners of kite. Tie the crossover with string. Make a hole in the centre of the kite and take one end of the string through to the other side. This end of the string should be about 2 in. long. Cut the other end off short. Stiffeners may be made from thin cane, Michaelmas Daisy stalks or coathanger wire.

Make a small hole in each corner of the kite outside the stiffeners. Thread a piece of string through a paper clip and tie in a loose loop through holes A and B, with paper clip on the face side.

Take string already coming through the centre and tie to paper clip with a thumb knot. This is the adjustment to improve flying performance. Tie this string to the flying string.

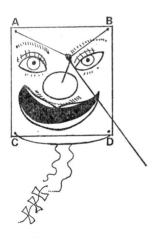

Fig. 5

Tie another loose loop of string through the two bottom holes C D. This is for the tail.

Make a tail by cutting a 3-in. length of crepe paper or plastic, or by tying little bundles of paper down a length of string.

POP-UP BOOK

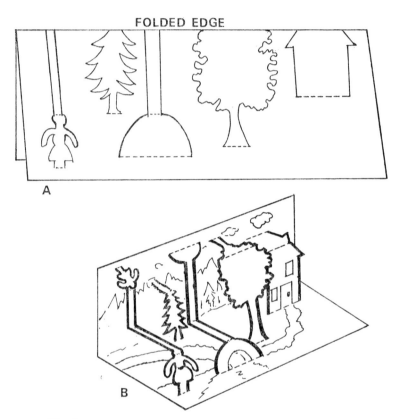

Fig. 6

Make from thin card.
Diagram A: Do not cut along folded edge. Score along dotted
lines. Open and push up objects.
The bridge and the figure have double folds.
The model is now ready to paint.
Pop-ups are fascinating and simple to make. There are many
ways of developing this into very complex movements.

PEEPSHOW AND THEATRE

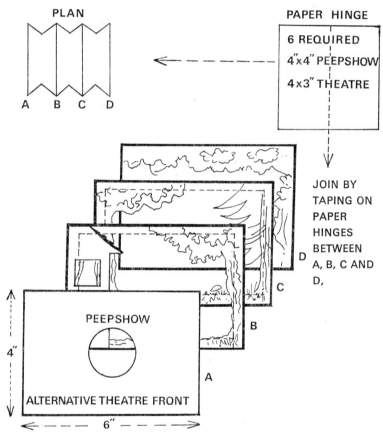

Fig. 7

A ½ in. hole for peepshow theatre front cut away as B C.
B Leave ½ in. frame all round as minimum.
C Draw on scenery round the edges and cut away centre.
D Back cloth is not cut.

some small G-clamps and sawing blocks, a bag of mixed nails and some suitable adhesive.

For whittling use assorted pieces of wood or pieces of root, which have more inspiring shapes than twigs. Driftwood can also be a source of interesting material. Having found a piece of wood with suitable shape and texture, use a knife and a rasp to shape, form and decorate the wood. The finished carving can be sealed with polish or coated with polyurethane, gloss or matt. To make a base, cut a strip of cardboard about 2 in. wide, bend it to a circular shape and fill it with plaster of Paris, holding it in place with an elastic band or string. While still wet bed in the carving and hold for a short while until the plaster sets, when the cardboard can be removed. The base can be left white or painted with black emulsion.

Construction offers opportunities for creating shapes and forms by joining pieces of wood together, a wide variety of off-cuts being necessary for this purpose. These creations may be in relief and inspired by the girder construction of modern buildings or the frame construction of old ones, by scaffolding, by atomic structures, by snowflake patterns, by hardware for space travel.

Scrapbooks compiled by children make useful reference books. These might come under various headings, for example people, plants, animals, buildings and machinery. Any work requiring detailed knowledge is best planned in advance so that pictures can be collected.

Scrap Materials. Classrooms should look like workshops and this involves having many materials available for the children's use. Among the egg boxes or tea chests sorted into various materials should be one full of cardboard shapes. There is such a variety of box shapes as well as tubes, discs and egg containers available. Add to this the various polystyrene tray shapes and packagings, the transparent and opaque polythene containers, children do indeed have a wealth of material from which to make models. If we augment this with off cuts of wood then most models are possible. A trigger tacker, stapler and impact adhesive make assembly easy.

Most card constructions are best painted with white emulsion paint first. This not only evens up the porosity and colour, but makes an ideal base for powder or block colour.

Carving. The tools already suggested under 'wood' may also serve for carving, with the addition of some 6 in. nails which make quite useful tools, and some screwdrivers or, if possible, stone carving chisels.

Plaster of Paris. This is a very good carving material and may be used in a number of ways. Random lumps of plaster are a good introduction to carving. A row of blobs of plaster about the size of the fist are placed on a sheet of newspaper. While these are still setting they should be pulled up to make as irregular a shape as possible and then left to dry. One of these will usually stimulate a child's imagination to see something in the shape, which can then be carved to make it more realistic.

Cylinders of plaster may be cast from cardboard tubes of various sizes, the tubes being removed when the plaster is dry. The plaster may then be cut up into slices and reassembled when carved as pieces of a totem pole. Similarly all kinds of plastic bottles can be filled with plaster of Paris and the bottle peeled off when the plaster has set, leaving shapes suitable for carving. For relief carving, slabs of plaster may be cast in polystyrene containers or seed trays, which have been greased first to prevent the plaster sticking.

With plaster, it is advisable to work on large sheets of agricultural polythene, or to work outside in summer.

Aerated concrete building blocks. These are ideal for carving as they can be worked with wood as well as stone carving tools. The blocks come in a standard size 9 in. x 18 in. but in a variety of thicknesses from 3 in. to 9 in. The thinner blocks are suitable for carving in relief and a number of them may be mounted on a base to make a large interior or exterior wall mural. The thicker blocks are suitable for carving in the round, and may be sawn, nailed, screwed or glued.

Polystyrene. Polystyrene can be obtained in both block and sheet form. Ceiling tiles are an example of small pieces, while larger sheets up to 1 in. thick are also available. It may be cut with a sharp knife, but is better cut with heat using one of the special tools made for the purpose. Shapes may be cut out and stuck together, but far more opportunities are offered by cutting into the surface with the special tools. When working in low relief on sheet polystyrene it is easier if it is stuck to a hardboard base. As the fumes are unpleasant one should be sure to work with cross ventilation. The finished work should not be painted with oil or cellulose paint as these are solvents. Emulsion paint is suitable and black will enhance the appearance of the work. When the emulsion is dry the work may be sprayed over with a metallic aerosol.

THE PRESENTATION AND DISPLAY OF CHILDREN'S WORK

The only value in showing children's work is as a bonus or seal of approval, as proof to colleagues and parents that the children are occupied with tools and paint, or to decorate the building. The value of work is in its creation.

As most schools are committed to display, it is often worth studying good shop window displays for ideas. Most rooms have display boards of one kind or another and work is best pinned to these with dressmakers pins, which are far less conspicuous than drawing pins and wherever possible, at the child's eye level.

Old picture frames obtained from junk yards and jumble sales can be very useful. Replace the picture and glass with insulation or pin board, which may be coated with white emulsion paint. Such a frame will set off a child's work to advantage, and also the work may be easily changed over.

There are, of course, many display systems available on the commercial market, and one of these is invaluable in order to maintain central display. So often school displays will not stand comparison with those of industrial or commercial organizations, which should not be the case.

Three-dimensional work is not quite so easy to display. A wooden box can be lined inside with wallpaper, shelved and hung on the wall. A collapsible stand can be made from $\frac{3}{4}$ in. blockboard (Fig. 8). 6 ft. high rolls of white or coloured corrugated paper may be obtained in 18 or 36 yard lengths. These make instant display possible as they may be run round a classroom and light work can be pinned on them.

Lettering presents its own problems, as it is usually too spidery and there is too much of it. Some of the modern letter faces used in magazines and on TV are worth copying. Children are subjected to the pressures of advertising and they are well used to modern lettering and display techniques. In many cases archaic lettering persists in school and is often out of context with the world that children live in.

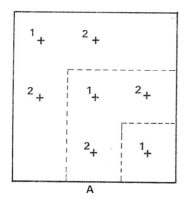

A

DISPLAY STAND

Cut a 4-foot square of ¾-in.
blockboard as diagram A. This
will make two L-shapes and a
square 16 in. wide.

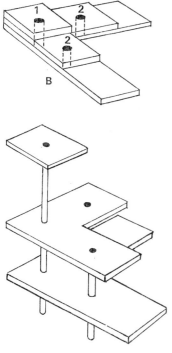

Place the three pieces on top of
each other as diagram B. Drill
holes through pieces as indicated
the diameter of a broom handle.

Cut one 2-ft. and two 1½-in.
lengths of broom stick. Drill
these down their length with
⅜ in. holes 3 in. apart. Cut
7 pegs from ⅜ in. dowelling
3 in. long.

Assemble stand as shown.
Adjust shelf height with pegs.

Fig. 8

THE EVALUATION OF CHILDREN'S WORK

How is children's work evaluated when so often their standards differ from those of the teacher? It will be considered heresy in many quarters to say that the standard of the end product is of minor importance, but to some extent this is true. It is the doing of the work, not the end product, which is of value. The experience a child gains in achieving the final result will vary through many factors. Gifted children will achieve much with little effort, the less able may make great personal effort with very little of this showing in the finished work. It is surely more important that children work to capacity and enjoy what they are doing. Encouragement is needed to give children confidence in their own abilities. Selecting the good and ignoring the bad will invariably do more good than the reverse. Work should be displayed for the children's benefit as well as the school's. If art and craft are a means of personal expression then failure cannot enter into it.

7

The Use of the Environment

DURING MY service at the Museum, there have been many instances with both young and adult visitors where some chance contact with a real object or event has aroused a lasting interest. An interest which, though often overlaid by circumstances, acts as a focal point of memory, so that even after a considerable period of time it can be recalled and all the old pleasure of discovery experienced anew. The children with whom this book deals are those who find abstract thought difficult and, therefore, there is all the more reason for giving them as much experience of reality as possible. Let us take, for example, the common frog.

A. The teacher tells the children what she knows about frogs. There are severe limits to both her description and also to understanding by the children.

B. The children read whatever books are available about frogs.

C. They also see drawings, illustrations in black and white and colour; film strips and slides.

C. This is followed by films, silent and sound, black and white or colour. Movement is very important; the frog jumps, its throat moves but its head does not; it croaks. The children see spawn and tadpoles; the interest increases rapidly.

E. The teacher shows a latex model of a frog and also perhaps enlarged models of tadpoles.

F. The teacher shows a live frog, spawn and tadpoles which may have been kept in the school vivarium.

G. The teacher and children visit a marsh and see frogs and other animals, e.g. newts and dragonflies in their natural environment.

You will agree, I think, that all these aids to understanding have their uses and any one or several may be available, but 'G' is really the most important and should always be tried. It should be realised that there are very many subjects and objects that may be concerned in studies of the environment.

Let us consider some of these for a moment. The writer's experience over many years with museums, universities, teachers, schools, societies and individuals suggests that a broad understanding, rather than a deep study of any one aspect of the surroundings, is of inestimable value to all of us, by increasing tolerance to all living organisms, engendering a feeling of belonging to the environment in which we live, and forming an understanding and sympathy for what has taken and what is taking place in the world at large.

Every teacher should acquire some intelligent grasp of the universe, especially because of the rapid advancement in space travel, radio and optical discoveries with modern telescopes. Parts of the Milky Way, many stars such as the Pole Star and the several constellations may be seen with the naked eye. Using a little ingenuity the children may be thrilled with facts and direct observation about, for example, the sun, some of the planets and their moons and the nearest real satellite, our moon. The recent visits to the moon by men call for attention. A model of the Solar System or a Lunar Calendar are within the capability of most schools. Field glasses and a small telescope are easily available. Meteors, so-called 'shooting stars', eclipse of the moon and the sun, are subjects for observation and study by teacher and children.

By day, observations may be made of the clouds and the colour of the sky, thunder and lightning, rain, hail, snow and the rainbow; the seasons; the winds and tides. The following are suggestions for study.

Solar system
On a sheet of expanded polystyrene about 3 ft by 2 ft by 1 in. draw the eclipses with a thick marking pen. Make the planets of Plasticine or polystyrene, with a bright one for the sun in the middle, and mount on pins or wires. The planets may be moved to show their relationship to the earth and the sun. Another way is to use a thin sheet of iron (tin) coloured black. The planets are mounted on short stalks each of which is fastened into the hole of little disc magnets; the orbits are painted as dotted lines. This board can be laid flat or hung up in the classroom.

Lunar calendar
Draw a circle upon a square of polystyrene about 3 ft by 1 in. and place the earth, a ball of about 3 in. diameter, upon a tilted axis of $3\frac{1}{2}°$. The moon is represented by a ping-pong ball on a vertical wire. The moon may be moved each day and flat pictures of the

phases as seen from the earth pinned on the board. Eclipses of the sun and moon can be demonstrated.

Weather
Arrange a cloud and weather observation week: draw clouds, measure rainfall; take temperature recordings.

Other suggestions
On the notice board put the time when artificial satellites might be seen passing across the sky. Give some explanation of space travel and the communication satellites for radio and television. Explain a 'shooting star' and borrow a real meteorite from the museum so pupils can see and handle it.

Other subjects for environmental study are the geography and contours of the local district, the rivers, lakes, marshes, hills and rocks. In this short account, one obviously cannot deal in any detail with the mass of potential material, but pupils can become fascinated with stones and minerals. The local environment has been modified and shaped into valleys and slopes by earth movement and the natural action of erosion and sedimentation. By making models, the reason for the meanders and the waterfalls may be explained. Of course, man has drastically altered the shape of the natural environment, which is an opportunity to emphasize and indicate how and why we should try to conserve the better part of our surroundings and not accept without protest the litter, pollution, noise and obliteration of natural beauty, destruction of historical sites and buildings.

A consideration of phenomena such as matter, electricity, magnetism, light, heat and sound may also be included, as these form part of the everyday environment. Although they are far too complex to teach to many children, it can be demonstrated that matter exists in three obvious states, i.e. solids, liquids or gases: refer here to ice, water and steam. There are many kinds of matter, some being pure, for example elements such as gold, oxygen or mercury. Some kinds of matter combine very closely with other kinds of matter, like carbon and oxygen (CO_2) which is part of the air we breathe. The air is a mixture of several gases; in order to emphasize this explain mixtures of sand and sugar, ink and water. Without confusing the children, explain how all matter consists of tiny particles, atoms, which are made up of even smaller particles, electrons, protons and neutrons. These particles are strongly held together or split apart by forces which are associated with magnet-ism and electricity. An electric current can be imagined as the rapid passage of electrons from one place to another along a conductor. A small battery and a torch bulb with a few inches of flex wire can help to demonstrate this. In a thunderstorm, there is a great rush of electrons from a cloud to the earth or from a cloud to another cloud. A piece of polystyrene shaped like a boat can be floated in a plastic bowl of water. Push an iron nail into the keel of the boat length-ways. Now let the pupils see the effect of bringing a magnet towards the bowl. Though not understanding the complexity of magnetism, they will be convinced that there is some attraction or repulsion between the magnet and the nail. This allows a compass to be intro-duced. The earth is a large magnet and the needle of the compass will always try to point to the north.

Expressions of energy like heat, light, radio-waves emanate from matter under certain conditions. A 'live' electric wire gives off heat. Much heat will make the wire glow white hot and the little wire in the bulb will give out light. Again draw attention to the torch and a soldering iron. The sun is enormously hot and is pouring out light, heat and energy all the time. Without this heat and light we could not live, and there would be no plants or animals on earth.

Another part of our environment is sound or noise. This is the result of the movement of atoms. Thunder is the effect of atoms moving in waves at a given frequency. Long waves make deep noises, short waves make high sounds like a whistle or a shriek. We hear conversation and music because of moving atoms striking the eardrums. The noise of jet aircraft, motor cars, road drills form the bad aspect of noise environment, but this is balanced by human voices in speech and song, music from wind, string and percussion instruments. It might be worthwhile to draw attention to the fact that extremely short waves cannot be heard but they can injure, while extremely long waves are associated with earthquakes. Sound waves cannot pass through a vacuum. Can a silent environment be imagined? What about deaf people?

It may not be apparent from above that man and all other living organisms i.e. animals and plants, are made up of associations of atoms. The matter of which we are made is wonderfully organised, for the world is full of countless kinds of plants and animals. We depend upon green plants to build up substances that we can eat and from which we get the energy to live. Trees have provided the material for buildings for ages past and also for fuel. Coal is the result of decaying vegetation that covered parts of the earth millions of years ago. Some fabrics for clothing are made from vegetable fibre for example, flax, cotton. Tea, cocoa and wine are all the products of plants.

From this brief introduction to the value of plants, interest may be extended by collecting and examining some of the common weeds, flowers and fruit. Hips, haws, blackberries, hazel nuts, chestnuts are all edible, but there are some kinds that are poisonous; examples are yew, nightshade, laburnum seeds. Many grasses are really beautiful and worth some attention. Cattle, producing milk, butter, cream and cheese, and sheep producing wool, feed almost entirely on grass. These animals convert grass into the meat upon which man partly depends to live.

The pattern of the leaves of many trees and shrubs can be further enjoyed by making moulds in plaster of Paris and colouring them. The leaves of the plane, sycamore, rowan and hydrangea are all excellent for their outline pattern of veins. Where facilities exist, or where they might be created, school gardens can be a source of much interest and value especially in cities. Small areas of flowers can be grown, also vegetables such as carrots, radishes and onions.

Let us now consider animal life. In the animal kingdom is a large field with which the pupils and their teachers may become better acquainted. The school aquarium and vivarium can provide opportunities to become familiar with such creatures as dragonflies, mayflies, water beetles, caddis flies, leeches, minnows, sticklebacks. The occasional outing with collecting nets and jars will engender a better understanding of ecology and environment. Gnats and mosquitoes can be reared in the classroom – giving the teacher the chance to speak of their effect on man throughout the world; how diseases like malaria and yellow fever can kill large numbers of people, or lower their standard of life. Greenfly, ladybirds, furniture beetles, caterpillars of butterflies and moths and their life histories can be examined. Many other kinds of familiar animals can be brought to the notice of the children. For instance, the economy of the honey bee can be described, perhaps with the aid of the school observation hive. Pupils can feed the birds, make nesting boxes, record the kinds of birds they see and also observe their nests and eggs. With a little help from the local museum, and practice, the wings and other parts of dead birds can be preserved and studied in the classroom. Although this is not a zoology course, it must be mentioned that in appropriate locations there are plenty of other creatures such as deer, foxes, badgers, otters, rabbits, hares, rats, mice, voles, shrews, bats, hedgehogs, moles, stoats and weasels. There are also snakes, lizards, newts, frogs, toads and fish to form material for our studies. Our environment does not only mean the study of wild creatures like those mentioned above as there are also domestic animals in the locality. In a cattle-raising area, what are the types of cows, are they raised for beef or dairy products? With sheep the kind of country, hilly, meadow or moorland, will affect the breed most suitable for wool or for meat. Pig rearing may be important in the economy of a district and may be associated with certain food crops grown near by. Perhaps racehorses are bred and trained on the chalkland; there may be a mink-farm for fur production in the valley, or rabbit rearing for its special fur and food value; chicken and egg production. In some districts there will be turkey farms and the breeding of pheasants, partridges, peacocks and other species of birds which in their own way all add importance in the study of a particular environment.

In many parts of Great Britain indications of occupations by pre-historic man are found. Hand axes of flint are dug out from the gravel terraces of rivers, for example, the Thames. These, con-temporary with extinct creatures like the mammoth and woolly rhinoceros, are several hundred thousand years old. Provincial museums will supply (on loan) these excavated tools and other archaeological material. On the downs or other high ground may be seen the remains of occupation sites of the neolithic culture and the tools used by the New Stone Age people.

The tumuli or long barrows are the burial places of the first Stone Age farmers. Their polished stone axes and chipped arrow heads are still being ploughed up in the fields or dredged from the bed of the Thames, where they were dropped from the primitive dugout canoes 2000 years B.C. Other materials, such as pottery, beads and Bronze Age swords and knives are not as numerous, but some are available for study in museums or often on loan to schools. Stonehenge and Avebury are monuments to these early ancestors.

Prehistoric periods continue through the Bronze Age, with its round barrows, into the Iron Age to about the period of the birth of Christ. The contemporary objects provide a mass of material and interest for teacher and pupil. Models of Bronze Age huts, Stone-henge, tools and pottery can be made in schools; pupils may be taken to visit archaeological sites being excavated in the surround-ing district. These visits may also be extended to include museums, art galleries, botanical gardens, zoos, country houses, farms, factories, shipyards and other places of interest. It may be difficult to arrange these out-of-doors activities but the educational value to the pupils is great.

Most towns will have houses of earlier periods, with characteristic styles of architecture, which may be compared with the dwellings on the modern housing estates. Teachers are advised to investigate their town noting the style of buildings, the groupings of houses, locations of high flats, areas of open ground, parks and playgrounds; the location of clubs and theatres, museum, art gallery or public library; the roads, the grass verges, the street lighting. Are there adequate pedestrian crossings; has the necessity of one-way traffic been explained; is there much 'through traffic' and are there reasonable facilities for short and long period parking of cars; are policemen and traffic wardens conspicuous or lacking? Have the multiple stores already taken over the main shopping centres; is public transport electric or diesel powered and is it reasonably adequate, with cheap or dear fares? The location of other public services is also of some concern. Is there an electric power station or gas works in the town; is the water supply from a river or a boring; how is refuse disposed? The main local industries such as coal, minerals, beer, biscuits, engineering, printing may be considered, and some attention might be paid to the huge blocks of buildings for insurance companies and banks. Is there a university and if so, has it special functions such as medical, economic, scientific, art or technical? Thus there is a wealth of material for environmental studies from which teachers and pupils can benefit by intelligent understanding and guidance.

Most museums now run a school service as part of their normal activities. The primary idea is to make many objects and replicas, covering the major subjects taught in schools, available for use in the classroom. Museums usually have large collections of material that for various reasons cannot be placed on view in the public galleries. The museum staff are also skilled in preserving, recording and displaying such objects. Local Education authorities share the cost of running the service, and where the scheme is developed, there is a provision for a service of vans to and from schools. From the comprehensive catalogue issued, teachers can request by phone, letter or personal call, any items for collection or delivery on dates arranged. Loans are normally for two weeks, but art material is lent for the term. Objects are grouped to form collections or items, and they are packed safely for transport and display, according to the nature of the material. Whenever possible, it is hoped and expected that pupils will be allowed to touch and handle the items. Where they are of too delicate a nature, for example, butterflies, the insects are mounted in transparent cases. Paintings are protected by glass frames but each picture has its own transport case. There is a great variety of objects available, covering such subjects as prehistory, history, geography, geology, zoology, botany, graphic art, ceramics, design, literature, astronomy, architecture, ships, locomotives, fabrics, films (16 mm), film strips, slides, microscope slides, gramophone records of plays and readings, music. Experience shows that objects are not damaged by handling by the pupils, this being a small worry compared with meeting demands or requests by teachers for more and more material.

From the above, it will be realised that the whole scheme is based on the belief that real objects or replicas have a very important place in educational and environmental studies, especially in primary schools. The complementary service to the lending of material to schools, is the visit by classes to the larger displayed collections, under the guidance of a teacher or a member of the museum staff.

8

Pastoral Care

STATE EDUCATION in Great Britain does not stand still. It adapts itself, cautiously, in response to the changing requirements of society and, in terms of curriculum, this adaptation has meant the inclusion of a progressively wider range of subjects. It is many years since proficiency in reading, writing and basic arithmetic was considered an adequate standard of education for the vast majority of people. Present-day schools provide more than a survival course in basic subjects in an attempt to give an opportunity to develop existing interests and open up fresh fields for the sake of the development of the whole child. But the whole child is far more than the part of him available for development at school – he was a whole child before he came to school.

It is becoming more and more apparent that the increased pace of modern life, particularly in cities, makes extra demands on children so that a further extension of school commitment is required.

Happenings in the home affect the child's behaviour in school and *vice versa*. Knowledge of the necessity to bridge gaps between home and school is the main reason for the increasing interest in the provision of pastoral care.

The fact that this chapter has been written indicates the recognition of the need to include consideration of the needs of the whole child in educational planning. How can pastoral care be defined? It is, perhaps, care first and foremost, care and caring for individual young people which prompts a teacher to get to know them and, in knowing them, to be aware of some of their needs and difficulties and to be ready to try to help.

Pastoral care is not a subject to be tackled in an allocated time, but is rather a continuing regard for the well-being of children and adolescents in school. The only limiting factor is the number any one teacher can care for in this sense. Nor is this a progress from one crisis situation to another, since where real rapport exists a child will often, as of right, take his problem to a teacher before it becomes large enough to be anything approaching a crisis situation.

Pastoral care has been practised in the special schools since their establishment. In this field much attention has been focused on the need to cater for the individual requirements of each child and to allow for individual emotional differences, and this policy has been continued in the special classes in junior and secondary schools. Children are placed in these classes as a result of existing difficulties or failure in general classes; this ensures that a certain amount of basic background information is available to the teacher from the start and the smaller numbers in special schools and special classes make for a closer child/teacher relationship.

In such a framework a wide-spread effort has been made to adapt the established requirements of school to the child's needs, rather than attempting to mould the child into the predetermined ways of the school. In this way the child benefits, not only from a programme of work geared to his own educational needs, but also from a social situation which allows, as far as is possible within a group setting, for his emotional difficulties.

The role of the teacher is now that of coping with the many and varied problems of exceptional children in these minority groups and providing far more than instruction. Links with the Welfare Services, School Medical Service, Child Guidance Clinics, Schools Psychological Services all add to the background information and help to build up a fuller picture of a child. In many cases the teacher is also practised in the use and interpretation of standardised tests so that a further source of information is available. Thus the background becomes clearer, but the foreground is the child himself, the product of these circumstances which are peculiar to him and inseparable from him.

Not all children in need of individual help are in special schools or classes. The difficulties and tensions of childhood and adolescence are common to most young people so that the risk of being bewildered and even overwhelmed is not confined to the educationally sub-normal, the physically handicapped and the maladjusted.

The child in any day school, is still the same being as the child who breakfasted at home (or maybe did not) and who will return at the end of the afternoon to his life outside school, to the community of which he is part and to whose standards and values he responded before first going to school. In some localities where community and school standards differ it may be wise for the school to be sufficiently sensitive to its pupils' requirements to adapt itself to the standards of its community and so ease the strain on pupils living in both surroundings. This can only be done if the school establishes and maintains close touch with its community by encouraging parents to come into the school and if members of staff are willing to go to their pupils' homes when necessary or when likely to be helpful.

A child brings his background to class as part of himself, influenced by parents, extended family and community and his learning will be in response to, and conditioned by, all aspects of his life, of which school is one. Some curricular developments reflect modified educational expectations geared to individual capabilities, interests and limitations. For instance, the Schools Council's Humanities Curriculum Project offers an opportunity for the group rather than the teacher to direct the course of discussion and investigation, drawing on ample provided resources in the form of written material, tapes, records, films and photographs, but considering opinions and ideas which are not imposed by the teacher.

It is not easy for the member of staff to abandon the role of instructor – nor is it easy for the pupils, although in the case of the Humanities Project they are the older boys and girls of 14 plus, to accept as genuine the change in approach. It is, however, much less difficult for all concerned when the teacher is already known, from past experience, to be understanding and ready to hear all sides of a question.

This type of project does not appeal to all members of staff any more than the pastoral care of a group is something to be undertaken by every teacher. There are many who maintain that welfare work should be left to the welfare services and that the teaching body should teach. Whether teaching and learning go together without well-being is questionable, that a great deal of such teaching will fall on deaf ears is almost certain. For the doubters perhaps the strongest justification for accepting the need to get to know children and adolescents as separate individual people and to be aware of the influences which at times cause stress, including those in the home, is that in strengthening contact and harmony between school and home those teachers who are willing and able to pursue this course do much to make the pupils more capable of benefiting from school life.

It would be wrong to imply that pastoral care had its beginning in Special Education. By tradition the local-headmaster has been regarded as the father of his school family. In village schools the school teacher has known and been known by the families of the children in the daily life of the village, so that contact has been natural and easy. In this setting pastoral care did not need a name, it did not figure as part of the requirements of a teaching appointment, it was carried out from day to day as part of the daily life, and the system remained unchanged as long as the schools were small units. With the advent of larger schools, however, the need for pastoral care increases, even out of proportion to the increase in numbers. Whatever the causes, and they are many, the needs are real and varied.

Who, then, in the big schools will be responsible for pastoral care? The house system, the year system, the faculty system all have their advantages and drawbacks but they all rely at base on a teacher getting to know about a group of pupils in a deep and real sense.

Not only can the head no longer know deeply and personally every pupil in school, but the teacher in charge of the house, or year, or whatever may be the system of groupings the internal organisation of the school produces, is also less closely in touch with individual pupils than those members of staff who are in day-to-day contact. The drawing together by the department head of relevant details is an administrative function and to some extent may counteract the lack of knowledge of staff, but it is not in itself pastoral care. The group teacher is the one most likely to undertake the pastoral care of that group.

Yet experience shows that long-term association often overrides such considerations as who is the form teacher; a child turns for help to the person from whom he has received understanding and communication and to whom he feels it is natural to go. Provided there are sufficient members of staff willing and capable of accepting and responding to such an approach there is little problem in helping and supporting the child who seeks help, for in bringing his difficulty to light he has made the first move towards its solution. But in the case of a child who does not make the first move, then who does? Perhaps it will be his parents who approach the school when they are themselves already troubled and anxious, and discussion and cooperation are long overdue. The teacher concerned will frequently have recognised the signs of difficulty and stress before this meeting and could have brought about discussion much earlier, either by inviting the parents to come to school at a time convenient to them, or, if this is not possible, by going to meet them at their own home. So often parents do not come to school because they are unable to leave the house, not because they are unwilling.

At the school in which the writer teaches pastoral care starts before the children come, when the head of Lower School visits the contributing Junior Schools and gains valuable background knowledge of those who are already experiencing difficulty. This is not a matter of pre-judging or being influenced by past situations but an attempt to avoid aggravating any existing problem or causing unnecessary pain. For instance, we know before the end of the junior school career that Mrs. X is a widow, perhaps newly so, and so the first letter which will go to that family does not go out addressed to Mr. & Mrs. X, and this letter will be sent before the child leaves primary school; or we know that a child will go into hospital during the summer holiday and may need much care and support in September.

During this same summer term all parents of prospective first year pupils are invited to come to school to meet the members of staff, and to be shown round the school before meeting as a group to be greeted by the headmaster and hear and discuss school policy and provision. Many doubts and confusions are sorted out on the spot, and many more are raised when the meeting closes and a large proportion of the people do not leave right away, preferring to wait for a private word. Later, in the last few days of term, the future first year pupils come from their primary schools and tour their new surroundings and meet the first-year teachers. In this way there will be a number of familiar faces on the very first day of the coming term, and a little of the sense of strangeness will be eased.

The next organised step comes in October when group teachers have had some opportunity of getting to know their children. All first year form teachers have a good opportunity for personal contact with each individual child since, in addition to morning and afternoon registration times, they teach their own classes for at least four periods each week. Every first year parent is now invited to a personal interview during an evening at a convenient time and date to discuss the child's well-being. At this early stage the emphasis is on welfare, and in most cases the interview is little more than an introductory conversation between adults with a common purpose. However, in a substantial minority of cases circumstances come to light, both medical and social, which affect the attitude and performance of the child.

It is not always easy for a parent to discuss family matters and children's shortcomings with a member of a school staff; some still regard the teacher as one of 'them', even in a situation where good school/community relations have been established. The authoritarian teacher is not a figure from historical literature – he or she is a remembered part of childhood in school for a great many of the people who today have heard of changes but have yet to be convinced, and some will quite rightly remain unconvinced.

The point must be made here that only very occasionally does a parent in such an interview disclose information in the expectation that it will not be passed on to any other person.

On the very rare occasions when parents feel there is need to give information of a very private nature, quite possibly not known even to the child, they almost always come to see the headmaster, deputy headmaster or senior mistress and the advisability of disclosure is considered then.

Certainly discretion is to be expected but in the great majority of cases if the matter is directly relevant to the child it must be passed to those actively concerned in the daily life of that child; this should be made clear to parents and their agreement secured. Accordingly, brief notes are made after the interview and passed to the head of Lower School who notifies those members of staff concerned and then files the information for reference if and when needed.

At the end of the first year the parents are again invited to a private interview after the school reports have been sent out. This gives the parents an opportunity, which most of them welcome, to discuss the report, the child's progress through the year and, in many cases, ask how they can help when support is needed. After a year the form teacher has far more knowledge of the child than at the first interview and can advise in these cases.

Each following year in the summer term an invitation is sent by the current form teacher so that regular contact is maintained, and by the time the third year interview arrives this will have been preceded by a meeting for all third year parents to discuss proposals for course work which will begin in the fourth year. From third year onwards interviews are increasingly concerned with preparations for career and examination requirements; these interviews are not in place of, but in addition to the meetings arranged by the careers staff in cooperation with the Youth Employment Officer.

There remain, of course, those who do not take up the invitation to come to school, and a little enquiry will in many cases show not an unwillingness, but an inability, perhaps one parent works in the evening and the other cannot leave young children, perhaps a physical disability coupled with lack of transport prevent a visit, and in these cases a teacher offers to go to the home at a convenient time, an offer almost always readily accepted. In such circumstances any doubts about the sincerity of the interest being shown soon disappear and a sound relationship is initiated.

Inevitably some families do not wish for such an association but resist it, and this must be accepted until a specific need arises.

This pre-planned framework of meetings by invitation is only the basic provision – the bulk of pastoral care is carried on in the normal course of events. Sometimes, from knowledge of a child, a teacher realises that school achievement is failing, or in general attitude and emotional response a child is strained, depressed, easily tired, excitable, and will then provide an informal opportunity for talk. Sometimes the approach is made, often very tentatively in the first place, by the child.

The member of staff concerned will not always be the registration teacher, it may be the young Physical Education staff or those who teach in another situation of active pupil participation such as, in the case of older girls, the Domestic Science staff, or again it may be any teacher who is accepted by the pupil concerned as being understanding and to be trusted. Clearly not every teacher wishes, nor should be expected, to be viewed in this light, and it is not an image to be presented from a sense of duty alone, for such a pose will not convince children and adolescents. To the duty-prompted attempt the child will respond only minimally, and then will answer along the lines he thinks the teacher wants to hear. The child's need for a spontaneous 'getting it off his chest' will not have been met and the teacher will have no clearer understanding of the pupil.

As previously mentioned, a great deal of pastoral care can fall to the Remedial Staff where special provision is made. Here the teacher is at pains to provide a programme of work individually planned to suit the educational needs of the pupil, but in formulating the work programme the whole child is taken into account and the background situations which may have given rise to the present difficulties are considered. It frequently happens that the teacher/pupil relationship formed here outlasts the period of remedial help, and even when the pupil no longer associates with the Remedial teacher for specified school periods he still regards that member of staff as the one most easily approached and most likely to help.

Whatever we mean by pastoral care, and it is not easy to define, it is not marking a register, catering for the visits of school doctor, nurse, dentist, sending out lists of school activities and finding lost property.

Parents today have become more content to leave much of the care of their children to other people and agencies, without enquiring very closely into the methods and activities involved. They are pleased to see their children occupied with Scouts, Guides, Youth Clubs, Sports Clubs, but show little interest in what they do there, nor inclination to help in the running of these activities. This is equally true of Parent and Teacher Associations; even a flourishing association can hope to rely on only a part of its membership for social events and on a very small section for active support on school and business matters.

Some parents are not sufficiently interested in discussing serious problems with their children to offer adequate time and patience, some children admit that their parents are unable to give them the help and guidance they seek. In circumstances such as these it is not difficult to see why young people look elsewhere than their homes for a lead at a time when they have little experience and inadequate preparation for assessing the worth of such a lead.

When adolescents show signs of unrest and confusion the public is inclined to look towards the school for a solution. Society is at a loss to find common ground on which to come to terms with young people with whom it finds itself out of touch. Almost all have been to school for at least ten years so that no other public service or social organisation has had such a widespread opportunity to influence them.

The home is surely the first influence but the home is changing. No longer is the family unit the main source of companionship and the centre of leisure-time activities. A considerable proportion of young people feel remote from their parents; they find difficulty in maintaining a close contact and in discussing viewpoints, queries and, especially, personal problems.

The family as a unit interlinked with a wider community retaining common bonds of interest, loyalty and affection was, in the past a strong framework in which the majority of children grew up. A child had an immediate source of comfort in his relations whenever he needed comfort and, with the extended family to draw upon, it was likely that someone would have time and sympathy to give when they were needed, and before the difficulty grew into a great problem. But such a group pre-supposes a stable community, as was the case, and to some extent still is in rural areas. Nowadays career considerations, both at parental and adolescent level, lead to the scattering of the family over a wide area. Communication with grandparents, aunts and uncles is frequently limited to pre-arranged visits and the steadying effect of talking things over without fuss and at the moment of urgency is gone.

For some youngsters an older sibling becomes the 'someone to talk things over with' who is a very real need in most lives, but not everyone has such a relative and the alternatives are few.

It is no longer realistic to suggest the local clergy since the influence of the church is declining, especially in respect of the over twelve-year-olds. It is true that many younger children still go to Sunday School, but their parents do not go to church. Without the expectation of continued church attendance with their families they do not develop the sense of fellowship within a larger family which formerly made the vicar a known, approachable and caring source of support and guidance.

The family doctor, too, is less of a 'family' figure. Large practices, group practices, leave little opportunity for a doctor to undertake this time-consuming care, and the doctor is added to the list of those who, no matter how willing, are not in a position to help.

In all these cases the teacher's main concern will be child-centred and for both child and parent a little practical help is always worth a lot of sympathy, but it is not always within the teacher's capacity to do more than listen. Where difficulties are so pronounced that a child is unable to adjust to life in school, or where consultation with his family indicates a need for further help the matter must be referred to the relevant Guidance and Welfare services.

Deprived children today are less likely to be hungry, ragged and physically uncared for than to suffer the deprivations of interest, communication and affection. They often feel out of touch with the world into which they are growing and so form groups among themselves, separate communities which tend to deviate further from the framework of adult society.

Young people are thrown back on their contemporaries and often attempt to sort out problems without help from any more mature person, even in matters of career and future.

Television programmes are often blamed for the attitudes of

I

children and adolescents, but families could use such material for discussion on social and moral issues. However, many parents shy away from this responsibility and their children, not surprisingly, are left to form their own opinions and standards without the modifying and balancing effect of discussion outside their own age group. Yet these same children, given the opportunity in school, are not unable to discuss. With encouragement they are often, either individually or in groups, well able to put a point of view to an adult and to seek support or listen to an opposing opinion.

Why, then, can they not discuss at home? Is it too much of an effort to talk above the sound of the television? Or is the programme of more interest to the family than the ideas and needs of one member of that family? Whatever the answer there is further evidence of a break in family social life.

In schools, also, there is a move towards a more impersonal situation and this is particularly so in secondary education. The films, film strips, closed-circuit television, teaching machines which can make for a far more vivid and, in many cases, enjoyable learning situation have their attendant drawback in their lack of personal quality. Yet personality and personal contact are the attributes of a successful teacher every bit as much as academic ability and professional expertise; and their influence spreads far beyond a teacher's own room, subject or classes. School children have a need for people and, to offset depersonalisation in teaching practices, they need teachers with whom to form relationships to create a sense of personal value in a sometimes impersonal situation. This aspect of pastoral care contributes both to the well-being and the development of the whole child.

Nowadays boys and girls mature physically earlier than was the case half a century ago and they are surrounded by a confused society of changing and conflicting views. One source of authority lays down one code, another, of equal standing, offers a contradiction, and in this confusion young people must formulate the standards for their own lives, a difficult course which must be allowed for in school if school is to be accepted as relevant to its pupils' lives.

The opportunity for discussion is not confined to any one subject or one teacher, many must have a part in the development of a whole personality. Planned discussions are already a part of, for instance, English and Religious Knowledge, and Domestic Science classes provide for smaller group discussion, but for many even a

comfortably informal group atmosphere is too public and an unob-
trusive private opportunity must be found which makes discussion
possible for the shy and the insecure as well as those whose problems incur a sense of shame.

The effects of behaviour difficulties resulting from personal
strain in only a few children may be felt by many others who associate with and react to them, so that the need for pastoral care in
schools is very real indeed since school is always there, it offers a
continuity and stability which may not always be wholly acceptable
to a child under stress, but it is at least constant and, it is to be
hoped, constantly available.

The difficulties themselves are, for the most part, the usual
problems of childhood and adolescence, i.e. conflict with parents
regarding hours, dress, appearance, boy or girl friends, behaviour,
pocket money, what to do in the evenings. They are problems
which, with understanding and communication in the home, can be
solved satisfactorily and an acceptable compromise reached. Where
such communication between the generations does not exist, the
child's view of his home situation may be distorted. In his eyes
parental unreasonableness is comprised of over-rigid control (or
inconsistency of control,) an unreasonable attitude to finance, unnecessary overcrowding, the cramping presence of an elderly or
invalid relative, the unjustifiable demands of a widowed parent, the
unfair advancement of a preference for a sibling, the unfair appor-
tionment of chores and, in the case of a wide spread of ages, older
children, particularly the girls, have too much responsibility at too
early an age and the youngest feel that too little time is given to
them.

Some of the complaints may well be justified but the view becomes more and more out of perspective so that the position is
exaggerated and the remark most likely to be heard is 'it isn't fair'.

Voicing the grievance will itself frequently be a relief, and calm
discussion with a teacher who is prepared to pay attention to the
problem without condemning the outburst will be of further help.
The subsequent approach to the parents will very often confirm at
least part of the child's claims, but it is equally likely to show that
his parents have been aware of and troubled by his attitude without
knowing what to do about it. For example, the child of strict or
elderly parents may be quite justified in claiming that he is being
treated like a much younger person, and a tactful approach by an
adult who is in daily contact with many other boys and girls will

often bring the views of the two generations a little closer together and help to gain some of the coveted privileges.

Frequently difficulties in school are capable of immediate partial solution after such discussion with parents: a child repeatedly failing to bring his homework to his teachers may well be unable rather than unwilling to do so because there is genuinely no quiet place in which to work at home. If arrangements can be made for the work to be done in his own time but on school premises the gain can be three-fold: the work is done, the child sees that 'they' have done something to help, and when he is no longer in the position of knowing he will be asked for work he has not done his resentment on that score will decrease. Further, his release from this particular strain may even have the added benefit of easing the home situation as well. Certainly nothing is lost and the home/school link is established.

Breakdown in communication between home and school comes when parents and teachers underestimate and fail to understand each other's role in dealing with cases of difficult behaviour. When a child seriously or repeatedly misbehaves at school the parents, more often than not, are asked to come to the school. The immediate implication is that they are being expected to make the child conform, that they are themselves to some extent being blamed. For their part, some will look upon a member of staff in much the same light as their own former teachers, that is, with a degree of awe and even fear and distrust, others will expect a police-type course of action to control anti-social behaviour. Some will regard the staff as experts in bringing up children and so expect them to do just that. Until a good relationship is established at adult level there is little foundation for happy and secure school life for children and adolescents.

The whole question of conforming to the requirements of school as a community is a source of discord where the aims of school conflict with the wishes of the family. It is possible that parents want their children prepared for a life as nearly as possible like their own. If the education received encourages attitudes and preferences too much at variance with parental inclination the parent/child communication will be hampered, not only by conflicting interests but in the very means of communicating, and stress and resentment are not the sole prerogative of the young. The manually capable son of an academic family and the artistic child of a labourer's family will have different interests from those of their parents but, less obviously, the gulf is not limited to the interests: modern methods in education lay stress on the ability to express oneself in words, and the more articulate younger generation may see its parents as dull and stupid. This is aggravating to youth – it is also distressing for the parents who can face considerable loneliness when they foresee their more educated children growing away from them. Envy and fear can then cause them to put difficulties in the path of their child and there is again a need for a closer communication with school.

School is no longer a closed community, we do not educate a child in isolation from home and social influences, and there is a need for parents to see school as it is today and for the school to cooperate with parents. Such cooperation can only be brought about by the efforts of the members of staff who know the school, its aims, its provisions and its people, and then only if those members of staff are prepared to move outside the school community and extend 'the school' to meet the families of its membership.

Knowledge of a child's background will in many instances bring to light the attendance at the home of visitors from other agencies who will be able to provide more information – or it may be that such visits are sorely needed and should be requested from the relevant organisations. Pastoral care of a teacher for a pupil will not be fully effective if, when difficulties arise, help that is needed for the family is not forthcoming. Once it is known that other agencies are involved consultation will avoid the aggravation of having too many people going to the house and will, in addition, bring to the school the support of experts in a different welfare field.

In the area in which the writer teaches an effort is being made to further cooperation between the agencies. In an experimental attempt to bring together as widely representative a body as possible invitations to meet have been sent to doctors, health visitors, district nurses, midwives, school nurses, child care officers, social workers, probation officers, careers officers, youth workers, clergy, nursery nurses and nursery nursing tutors and teachers in Colleges of Education as well as teachers in schools, special schools and further education establishments.

Meetings take the form of non-structured informal discussion aimed at investigating differing approaches, purpose, specific areas of concern and viewpoint brought to bear on the common concern, young people. Either specifically or included in a wider social group all the departments of official provision represented in this list work for the well-being of children and adolescents, if and when the need for their services arises. At the moment the tendency is to remain in separate compartments with vested interests, and it is hoped that discussion and understanding of other related philosophies will help to bring about a greater degree of liaison between different branches of what is, in effect, an uncoordinated social service.

So far the experiment is in its very early stages and it is apparent that all have a great deal to learn from colleagues. Whereas there already exists a degree of collaboration and pooling of knowledge in the more obviously allied services, it is by no means a foregone conclusion that this collaboration will be extended without a great deal of re-thinking, adaptation and change of attitude.

The question inevitably arises, 'Do we accept the premise that those working with people, with the intention of influencing their lives, should work as a team?' If so, coordination is necessary and who will coordinate? It is easy to say we must break down barriers but not so easy to say how it is to be done, what skills are required; what indeed we mean by 'care' and how we act in a caring situation. What is our responsibility to the individual? Do we know what we mean by responsibility, both legal and moral?

It is, of course, one of the purposes of the experiment to recognise and challenge the barriers and suspicions which we all realise do exist, we who are teachers must be aware that many of these barriers stand between the teaching body and other agencies. If this is the result of the school experience of those who are now adult and themselves concerned with young people, then the teachers of twenty or thirty years ago have a great deal to answer for.

Whatever the reasons it is clear that much more than lip service is necessary. Cooperation cannot be achieved merely by talking about it.

It would no doubt be very convenient if a clear distinction could be made between pastoral care and counselling. If we could say, 'up to such and such a point we are talking about pastoral care and beyond that point we refer to counselling.' But there can be no demarcation line which will be applicable to any number of instances. Pastoral care and counselling, both terms capable of widely varying definitions, are closely interlinked and synonymous in some areas. On the one hand, pastoral care is compatible with the traditional professional aims of the good teacher, and will, on occasion, include aspects of counselling. On the other hand counselling has a more structured framework which will include some aspects of pastoral care. Teachers, school counsellors and social workers all operate on a basis of first recognising a need for help and then taking steps, but many differences may well lie in the choice of steps.

All three approaches are based on the assumption that the individual has worth in himself, regardless of the pattern of his behaviour, and that it is possible to develop what is worthwhile in that individual because he has a potential for development. The problem facing teachers, school counsellors and social workers is to uncover the root cause of the child's difficulty or distress.

The approach of the counsellor and the social worker will be based on the belief that within the accepted standards of the society in which he lives the individual has the right to solve his own problems. The counsellor has to allow his client freedom of expression without fear of censure. He will maintain this attitude even when his own maxims are attacked but the teacher, because of expectations and the need to share his concern fairly between other members of the group and the individual, will often have to be prepared to exercise authority. His is the difficult, if not impossible, task of reconciling the two roles. This may well be the justification for the separation of these two functions; yet without the close knowledge of school, which can only be gained by working in it, how can guidance, which is an essential part of the counsellor's job, have any real value to pupils and parents seeking guidance in home/school matters?

Whether a distinction can be made between care for a child in his capacity as a member of a school community affected by background influences, and care for him as a member of his family and social group affected by school influences is a very debatable point. Whether there is any clear line between pastoral care and counselling is debatable. What is definite is that the pastoral care of a teacher for a child should start at the beginning of their association, in the firm conviction that every child needs to know that he is cared for whether he has particular problems or not.

9

Education for Personal Relationships

THE TEACHER was reading the story of Goldilocks and the Three Bears to the first class of a special school for E.S.N. children. They knew the story and were preparing to dress up and act it after the reading. Parts had been allocated and the little actors and actresses were listening intently and commenting at intervals. At the end of the story the teacher asked 'and what would happen if Goldilocks disobeyed her mother and father and went into the woods again by herself?' 'She'd get a clip round the ear 'ole' was Goldilocks' swift reply.

A child, no matter how backward educationally, understands and responds to the family pattern of relationships. If one thinks of any class in any school, normal, remedial or special, the family life of each child, if studied and described in anthropological terms, would reveal a number and variety of child-rearing and marital customs sufficient to fill a large volume. The family is the training ground for the art of personal relationships and many would assert that there is little to be done after the child reaches school age. This is obviously not the view of those now working in the field called 'Education for Personal Relationships', 'Education for Family Life', 'Social Education', and many other titles used to describe efforts to help children grow socially and emotionally as well as intellectually. Nor is it the conviction of all those who are now energetically promoting a wide range of counselling services in schools.

Goldilocks' teacher certainly, at the very beginning of the child's school career, demonstrates clearly to the child that there are other ways of achieving cooperation and obedience than by 'a clip round the ear 'ole.' Throughout the child's life, through relationships with other significant adults, with the peer groups, he will discover many different ways of interacting with other people. The object of any deliberate teaching of 'personal relationships' is not to change the child's expectations and manifestations of behaviour into a teacher's preconceived and probably middle-class pattern, but to help each child to assimilate and practise for himself those dealings with others which will afford him the most satisfying and helpful experiences.

We cannot escape from value judgements, but we should at least be aware of our own conditioned beliefs, prejudices and enthusiasms. One may accept as good those relationships with others which promote harmony and cooperation while condemning those which lead to exploitation, bullying or over-dependence. In short, love is better than hate, but love is not smothering or over-protection. Good behaviour may be merely the keeping of the rules; consideration for others is revealed in good manners, but morality in relationships involves choice. Helping children to grow up calls for careful evaluation of the child's readiness and ability to exercise choice at each stage of development. Rules made for a young and dependent child need to be changed as the child begins to ask 'why?'. The prohibition against playing with matches changes into instruction in the lighting and control of fires.

Where the backward child is concerned, the need for protection lasts longer, the area of decision-making remains circumscribed for a longer period, and the ability to use initiative may be delayed.

When we are dealing with a child who is educationally backward in a remedial class, we cannot assume that he is socially retarded. For example, Jimmy, who is eight and cannot read, is expert at finding his way about on trains and buses. He is also a skilful thief and the ringleader of a small gang, who regularly play truant. No lack of initiative as far as Jimmy is concerned! Another slow learner, Mary, takes full charge of her brothers and sisters, and her mother entrusts her with the money and responsibility for the family shopping. Mary is wise and competent in baby care, yet at school she remains among the dullest in the remedial class.

Many other examples could be described of boys and girls who are capable and confident in some areas of living, while deemed 'backward' educationally. The necessary simplifications of method used to help such children to read and write are often found in textbooks which are too childish in content. Recently, books have been published which present more relevant and acceptable material in simple form and vocabulary, and it is to be hoped that more reading centres similar to the one at Reading University School of Education will be opened to assist teachers in their choice of books and other modern aids.

The 'restricted code' of the backward child may sometimes conceal a wealth of knowledge and experience, gleaned from home and neighbourhood and late night television. This social information is not always accessible or acceptable to teachers who may have led more sheltered lives.* On the other hand, children from more favoured homes may express themselves in the 'elaborate code' of the educated classes, but their range of understanding of different social conditions may be narrow.

Social skills such as Mary's give confidence, which may often counteract a child's sense of failure, when he is in the low stream or remedial class at school. Some schools increase the child's feelings of rejection or despair through their over-emphasis on academic success. Rigid streaming often results in the 'self-fulfilling prophecy' and it is not surprising to find many 'Jimmies' building up a false sense of identity and power through delinquency, to cover and disguise their true feelings of inadequacy and hopelessness. Other children may cloak their despair with apathy.

The teacher's difficult task is to promote the confidence that encourages the effort to learn, and the hope of achievement that carries one through the inevitable drudgery of practising any skill or craft.

However dull academically, sooner or later a child becomes a wage-earner, most likely a husband or a wife, a parent and a citizen. These stages in their lives may not be chosen at the right time or in the right order in the opinion of parents and teachers, and although it is usually assumed that parents will guide and advise their children as they take on adult roles, increasingly the schools are expected to provide vocational guidance, sex education and preparation for marriage, parenthood and citizenship in a world of rapid and bewildering change.

As the school leaving age is raised, we find that those we describe as school-children are physically fully adult. The climate of our time seems to bring them the freedom, the money and the temptations that were scarcely available to wage-earners of the same age in previous generations. It is not long since most youngsters went to work at the age of twelve, yet now that the law recognises the adult as fully responsible at the age of eighteen, we have an increasing number of men and women of that age still at school. Erik Erikson writes 'It is human to have a long childhood; it is civilized to have

* In a survey done in Bristol University among 3,500 teachers in their first posts, 4 in 10 of their head teachers mentioned 'unfamiliarity with the child's social background' as a cause for concern (quoted by Nicholas Bagnell – *Sunday Telegraph*, June 31, 1971).

an ever longer childhood. Long childhood makes a technical and mental virtuoso out of a man, but it also leaves a lifelong residue of emotional immaturity in him.' For all children, no matter how bright or how dull, it is this emotional and social development of the personality that is coming to play a major part in the planning of a curriculum that will be relevant to the needs of today. Subjects taught under the umbrella of 'Social Studies', 'The Humanities', and so forth do not affect the social and emotional growth of the boys and girls, unless teachers encourage learning through methods which involve personal interaction within small groups, and with people in the environment outside the school. Projects which include excursions, fact-finding explorations, group work, team teaching and above all, informal discussions are acceptable and stimulating to young people, but such methods make heavy demands on the teacher's initiative and energy. Fortunately many experiences are now described and suitable literature and other aids are available.

The child's natural curiosity, which is the mainspring of learning, may lead to unexpected fields. The teacher may be quite unprepared for the topics that may arise during informal discussions. 'Let's find out together' is perhaps a most fruitful learning situation, but it takes a mature and confident teacher to put aside the role of all-knowing fount of wisdom. Still more maturity and skill are called for to listen to young people; to pay real attention to what it is they are trying to say, to 'listen with the third ear' for the undertones of anxiety, to encourage the expression of muddled thoughts in a very limited or even unacceptable vocabulary. The attempt to speak in a manner expected in the classroom often inhibits the flow of expression. A child is often silent in the classroom because he cannot speak correctly, but watch him in the playground with his chosen mates and he is never at a loss for words. In large classes it is difficult to give each child sufficient time and opportunity to express himself verbally, yet most of our social life depends upon verbal communication. Indeed, many of the misunderstandings and tragedies in life – in friendship, in working relationships, in love and in marriage, come about through lack of the ability to make feelings understood, and to put clearly into words the tensions and worries, the fears and doubts that bedevil relationships and block progress in mutual comprehension.

When large classes are broken into small groups for projects, or visits, there is a need to communicate, to pass on instructions, to prepare reports, to compare findings, all of which help to increase social competence. These new methods are in striking contrast to the time-honoured arrangement, whereby sitting in serried rows, looking at a teacher through the backs of other people's heads makes communication impossible. Training young people to sit still and keep silent may help them to adjust to factory conditions, where each one must work steadily at his allotted task; yet nowadays, in modern factories, conditions increasingly provide for job-satisfaction through better facilities for consultation, communications and diversion. Training for factory conditions may be a necessary part of education, but training and education are different processes. When we speak of education for personal relationships we do not mean training, although we need not ignore the need for conventional manners and forms of conduct suitable for different occasions. Indeed, one finds that children appreciate lessons dealing with such matters as how to give a party, the correct way to receive guests and effect introductions, the study of the menu and the use of cutlery in a restaurant. Committee procedures, dress and manners suitable for an interview when seeking employment, buying and selling in shops and wholesale warehouses, the reception of a professional worker's clients, visiting the sick or aged, asking favours, writing letters to important people – all these and many other situations may be discussed. Many teachers successfully use techniques such as role-playing, drama, mime to induce confidence and skill. All this may seem more like social training than social education, and the differences will depend largely on the teacher's attitudes. Social training may be all that is required when lives are rigidly circumscribed, and where each child may expect to assume a role allocated to him in a tight family circle. Social training is of course the highest goal for some severely subnormal people. Nowadays, social training can help a child to live more easily in a flexible society; to accept the geographical and educational mobility by which people change their mores, move into different classes and professions, meet people from other lands and walks of life – and feel at ease.

However, in a changing world, social training is certainly not sufficient. Strong feelings are aroused by changes of any kind. Goldilocks will have feelings about her teacher, and her teacher's attitudes will cause her to question the family patterns. If the family is from another country, the comparisons will be even more striking and often the cause of tension and unhappiness. There are many examples of girls for whom marriages are arranged at the earliest possible age, when the girl herself is just finding an interest in education for a career. It is painful for any child to find the family wanting in understanding, yet to be misunderstood is the common fate of adolescents, and it is during these painful years that teachers are the important figures around which feelings about authority will be developed and understood. Teachers should be aware that what they are is more important than what they say, and that what they are is made obvious by what they do. Their actions are felt by the child as a measure of their concern for the child. Children know only too well if they are loved, valued, or disliked and rejected. The child's feelings about himself will be enhanced for good or ill by the teacher's attitude. Obviously no human being can love all children equally. No teacher could be kind, sensitive, understanding and warmly encouraging to every child every day. Many children have been so wounded that they are unable to trust any adult or accept sympathetic treatment, however tactfully offered. The wonder is that there are so many good teachers able to treat every child with the respect that is the right of every human being. Most good teachers accept and work at their pastoral role and of course, in remedial classes this is the most important aspect of their work – to find and promote the growing points of each child's capacities. In many cases teachers make great efforts to understand the child in his own frame of reference through meeting the parents, visiting the home, cooperating with school welfare workers, local social workers and others from the Child Guidance Clinics or Local Authority services. Indeed, one teacher in a secondary school asserted that he could not teach his class unless he had visited every home, and this he managed to do at the beginning of each school year. Not many would find time and enthusiasm or the suitable environment where this might be possible, but most remedial or special class teachers encourage parents to visit frequently. Open days and parents' meetings, parent-teacher associations, case conferences, all help, and it is amazing to see how a teacher's attitude towards a difficult child may change when through her own visit or a description from a social worker, she discovers the emotional and social reasons for the bad behaviour and the inability to attend to lessons. Alec Clegg and Barbara Megson give us some estimate of the number of children in distress and the agony that many endure at home. (See reference list.)

In teaching relationships, it is important to realise that there are dangers even when the teacher achieves successful relationships with the children. However unsatisfactory the parents, they are the most important people in the child's life and the teacher must be careful not to drive a wedge between the child and his family. A wise teacher does not derive satisfaction from hearing a child say 'I wish you were my Mummy' or 'my Daddy'. This a possible danger signal, perhaps a starting point for discussions of family life, its trials and tribulations, difficulties about housing and money which are the lot of too many people, as well as the delights and the fun of family life. A child may be cunningly seeking to curry favour with teacher, in a temporary mood of affection, or he may be in real trouble and needing the quality of love and care that a teacher cannot possibly give, or there may be a need for psychiatric or counselling help. It is to be hoped that there will be more facilities for the services that are needed in all schools, not only to help the needy children, but also to assist the teacher in understanding the distress signals that appear in the classroom.

The child's feelings about himself, his own self-image, are the foundations upon which he will build his feelings about other people. One must first love oneself before one can love others as oneself. Too many children have their own self-esteem warped from early childhood by the lack of security and warm, loving acceptance. If a child is in a remedial class or special school, he will know that he is different from other children. He may need help in accepting himself as he is and making necessary efforts at adjustment. Parents may react irrationally, they may feel aggrieved or guilty, thus making life even more difficult for their child. They may refuse to recognise a defect and so make life more painful for a handicapped child. A social worker may help the child most by working with the parents. Broken homes, unhappy couples, poverty, ill-health, mental defect and mental illness, addiction to drink, drugs or gambling – all of these conditions in the home may mark a child for life. School, however understanding and kind the atmosphere, can only modify the damage, and yet, through good teachers who can make a child feel valued and accepted for himself, many fine characters have developed in spite of adversity. It is through self-understanding and the gradual assimilation and use of experience, however painful, that early disasters and difficulties may be overcome, and in this process, a wise and loving adult may mitigate the lack of an affectionate family background and pave the way to a sense of real achievement through appropriate school studies.

Self-esteem must be based upon a positive feeling about one's own body. If the upbringing has imposed restrictions upon mobility and free play with suitable toys, and material such as water, earth and clay, a child may either behave in a wild and uncontrollable fashion when he is first allowed space and freedom, or he will lack the exploratory drive and initiative necessary to develop skill in the use of his limbs and his senses. Too many children are brought up in shared houses or small flats, where every natural movement, cry, laugh or song is prohibited through fear of annoying the neighbours or the landlord. Natural functions of the body are often considered wicked or unmentionable. 'Naughty, dirty, don't touch' or 'Don't you dirty those clean clothes!' are frequently the daunting reactions to a child's attempts to find out about himself and his environment, and to use his own powers with confidence. In his regular activities, the child betrays clues to his feelings about himself by his posture and movements. A sensitive approach through physical education, music and movement and drama or art can be more valuable than psychiatric intervention in some cases. One sees many little children unable to relax or breathe easily.

A child is often made to feel guilty about his sex organs. These are not to be named or touched after the nappy stage is outgrown, yet early in school or even nursery school life, they are the subject of shameful sniggers. Even the child from a family which uses an appropriate vocabulary learns in his first year at school to giggle about 'bums' and 'titties'. What are the teachers' attitudes? They too will have been conditioned by their own upbringing, but in the classes of the youngest children, one sees how attitudes are formed, and it is therefore in the early years that these may best be modified. It is because adults, like children, find it hard to shed or change the attitudes that parents pass on to them, that we find confusion about sex education. Most adults carry through life some hang-ups or inhibitions about sex, making not only for difficulty in talking about a subject which is after all common to all humans and animals, but more sadly, the effect of such childhood conditioning reaches into marriage and sexual relationships later in life. When parents are confused, unhappy or mentally disturbed, or all of these, consequences may be disastrous for children.

Linda and Bill come from such a home. Bill is eight and Linda is six. Bill's teacher, in answer to questions in class told the children that babies grow inside their mothers (there are many suitable books for Primary School Children). Shortly after, Bill came to

school one day in a more than usually dirty and malodorous condition, so much so that a member of staff gave him a bath. She
noted horrid weals on his back and reported this to the Head. A
home visit was arranged and the school welfare officer told the
story. At home, during tea, Bill had said to his sister, 'You came out
of Mummy's belly, like me.' Mother told the visitor that she was
shocked and upset by this dirty talk and had asked her husband to
beat Bill for his wickedness! Case-work help was fortunately available for this family, and many difficulties were uncovered leading
to Bill's transference to a boarding school away from father's
cruelty.

This is an extreme case, and such incidents, and many less
serious ones, could be avoided by closer contact with parents, or,
in the case of those parents who never come to the school, some
means whereby parents might be prepared, when a child first
enters school, to face the fact that the truth will be told in reply to
all questions. It seems almost incredible and impossible in this day
and age, when the mass-media purvey the most lurid and vivid
details of sexual behaviour, and when almost every child lives with
a television set in constant operation in the home, that parents can
still feel uncomfortable, or object when human biology is taught
in school.

Their cooperation may be enlisted when some thought is given
to the subject by heads and staff. Films and television programmes
used in school may be shown to parents, helping parents and
children to communicate more easily at home. Parents with objec-
tions or anxieties usually need help, and should be asked to visit the
head. Parents' permission is not asked about any other subject
which heads put into the time-table, but a great fuss is often made
about sex education. Rumours spread through the Town Hall and
in the local press sex is always 'news'. Children are not blind or
deaf, and are quick to realise that our bodies must be understood
before we discuss our feelings and ideas about relationships with
other people. It is for the parents to keep ahead of their children,
with the help of the teachers.

It is only when children grow up without false shame in an
atmosphere of truth and honesty, that sex finds its proper place.
Undue and unhealthy curiosity is often the direct result of the
thwarting of natural curiosity of the young child. When the response to awkward questions is 'Not now, dear' or 'Wait till you are
older', or 'Mother's busy'. When the child meets with laughter or

ridicule, or untruthful or facetious replies curiosity goes under-ground. When adults cannot be trusted to tell the truth or to ex-plain and discuss, the child believes the misleading and dangerous things he hears from other children, and mysteries remain to frighten and worry, perhaps for years. Unsolved problems and the repression of the desire to learn the truth, may have serious repro-cussions upon the future capacity to enjoy a healthy lovelife, as marriage counsellors often discover.

The sexually titillating rubbish now so widely available in shops and on bookstalls, is surely there in response to a demand created by curiosity repressed in childhood.

Few people have written about the sex education of the handi-capped child. The child who knows that there is something wrong with him, either mentally or physically, will feel unattractive and may have difficulties in making friends. There will be obstacles in developing relationships with the opposite sex. When more institutionalised patterns of care and education were the rule, the sexes were kept apart – a sure way of dealing with their vulnera-bility. Now that the care of the backward youngster is increasingly coming within the responsibility of the schools and the community, with its wider freedom, one is forced to consider not only how to provide essential sexual knowledge, but also how best to help each child to find a suitable framework for his own conduct.

The parent or teacher who responds immediately and appropri-ately to a child's question, will play an important part in inculcating healthy attitudes to the body and respect for the self. The friendly adult with time and availability when a child displays a need, becomes a particularly valuable guide and example to the child whose parents do not provide a happy model.

Guidance was once firmly grounded in religious beliefs. Fear, too, often played an important part in behaviour. What motives do we find today? There is nothing new about widespread greed, hedonism and competition. Modern technology enables more people to join the affluent society, and football pools, betting shops, bingo and television, play a larger part in family life than prayers or church attendance. 'What's in it for me?' 'He only does it for the money', 'As long as I'm all right' are the motives emphasised in the mass media and in general conversation, and yet altruistic feelings and pursuits pervade the schools and youth groups to a remarkable degree. Even among the backward children, one finds great efforts to help those even more handicapped than they are themselves.

At the present time, the average age for marriage is lower than it has been for several generations. Young people rush into the responsibilities of marriage and parenthood. Love and security in personal relationships, are like dominant motives as they have ever been. The haste with which these responsibilities are assumed may be deplored by the older generation, but possibly this very eagerness often reflects the lack of secure relationships in family, school and friendships, and the false hope that mature affection comes with marriage instead of through long preparation through many kinds of relationships. In conversations with boys and girls in all types of school, one finds them looking forward to marriage – hoping to achieve loyal and lasting affection, and wishing to provide this for their own children.

No school day is without many opportunities to promote the good relationships so ardently needed and desired. Even the most backward child can distinguish between consideration and rejection, cruelty and kindness, whether in school, in stories of real life or in fiction. There is nothing new in pointing out the consequences of loyalty or betrayal, truth or falsehood. The child, as he grows up in a changing world where a bewildering kaleidoscope of ideas and values present him with a wide range of behaviour, will inevitably have to choose a pattern of living for himself. How he regards and treats others will depend upon the way others have treated him.

Teachers and parents find boys and girls who conform or rebel at different stages in their development. One child may be obedient at home and at school, another may defy only a parent, or reserve hostility for teachers, or perhaps one particular teacher at one particular time. The motives will depend upon relationships; is the child seeking approval and love from admired or feared adults? Is the defiance a reflection of an inner need to find an identity, or is it in response to intolerable frustration, or a lack of opportunity to use potential talents?

In all cases one may see how training given in the home may be reinforced or modified in the school. The child who trusts and loves at least some adults is in a position to choose how far he will allow his behaviour to be influenced by his peers. The child who is 'weak and easily led' has usually lacked a strong lead from meaningful adults. The backward child who is also deprived of good parental example is exceptionally vulnerable and most likely to be led astray in sexual matters, mistaking any casual interest for genuine affection. Only sound education from teachers who can make a good relationship will protect such a child. In extreme cases, the discerning teacher will know when to apply for expert help.

As we have seen in the case of Goldilocks, child and parent react to each other according to the family culture. Where this behaviour is consistent, the child is at least not confused. Where relationships are good, no matter what the pattern may be, behaviour is increasingly dictated by reason and this is the measure of the child's social and emotional growth. As the child grows older, he can understand the parents' reasoning as well as his own, and cooperation gradually replaces blind obedience or open or furtive rebellion. Even after the seemingly inevitable periods of revolt, whether young people agree with parents' values or not, most of them agree that parents exert the greatest influence in their lives. The majority of young married couples after all seem to model their family life upon the parents' example, most often seeking their advice and help.

Where we find good personal relationships based upon mutual love and respect, sexual relationships may be expected to follow the same pattern. If there is no open discussion of personal feelings, of sex in its widest terms as it affects roles in society, the capacity to give and receive love, the ability to assume responsibility for oneself and others, we may leave young people well informed about a great many matters, yet leave them ignorant and vulnerable in the area of sex.

When there is no lead from adults even brilliant and gifted scholars are as vulnerable as the backward; indeed often more vulnerable since the young person under severe academic stress sometimes seeks escape or release in a realm of unthinking sensation or emotion.

What every child needs at all stages of growing up, are mature and honest adults, willing to answer questions simply and directly and as soon as they are asked. Such adults should help the child to learn to live in the world as he finds it around him, and should not shirk the puzzling aspects of conduct and behaviour that are presented to the child in his everyday contacts; at home, in the streets, in newspapers, cinema, television and radio.

Ideally, these adults should be the parents, yet in a fairly recent survey, of young people between fifteen and eighteen, only 27% of the girls and only 7% of the boys had had any help or instruction from parents about the relationships between the sexes (Schofield).

It must be remembered that for many parents their own relationship is far from loving and satisfying. How then can they be expected to convey healthy attitudes to their children, no matter what they say? Teachers often suggest that only married people should give sex education to children, but a bitter and hostile wife or husband may gave a false and harmful view of life, while an idealistic and warm-hearted unmarried teacher may be of the greatest help to a child. Similarly, an older person who has learned through experience to come to terms with loss, frustration, divorce or widowhood, may have the wisdom and compassion that is invaluable in dealing with children.

Married or single status has little to do with the ability to teach personal relationships successfully. The personality of the teacher is considered to be of first importance and therefore, many local authorities now provide not only courses for teachers on Education for Personal Relationships but also a personality selection test. In some instances, teachers are first recommended for the course by their headteachers and then have to undergo a selection procedure. In some local authorities, a self-selection process takes place during the training course, since self-insight is the key to awareness and sensitivity where the children are concerned.

Teachers often need to work at their own embarrassment. This is sometimes more closely allied to vocabulary than to subject matter, but a sense of humour is essential along with the ability to deal with fun, ribaldry and exhibitionism in the classroom. The most helpful means of developing the personal qualities needed when education seeks to encourage social and emotional growth, is the regular discussion group. These may be organised within a school, or by a local authority, the marriage guidance council, or child guidance team. The team of teachers involved in the project should attend together, with the support and encouragement of the head. Good interpersonal relationships within the school are a prerequisite and where these obtain, teachers who have completed the in-service training find that there is no need to call in any outside speakers or specialists.

When one bears in mind the different needs of individual children in remedial classes, it is obvious that talks, lectures, films or discussions led by outside visitors may not always be as successful as the everyday work of good teachers who take each child's questions as they come. The child may need a brief factual answer to a specific question, a more detailed explanation of physiological matters, a discussion about behaviour or moral standards, or prolonged counselling about a serious problem.

There are some difficulties that call for the kind of counselling or psychiatric help that might conflict with the teacher's role – the teacher must be aware of the limitations – but every school ideally should have its own social worker or counsellor. Good liaison with the new social services committees should ensure speedy help when needed.

Every teacher teaches in his or her own way, and in every school conditions vary. Numbers of children in remedial classes are often impossibly large and specialist training not always easily available. Local authorities may be sympathetic and generous to their handicapped children, but in some areas, the opposite is the case. It would therefore be presumptuous to suggest a syllabus, or project methods, suitable for all remedial classes. Instead, it might be helpful to look at the questions asked and topics discussed whenever lecturers or counsellors introduce personal relationships as the theme.

No matter how well human biology has been taught, children do not absorb information until they are ready to receive it, and many are blocked by emotional problems which prevent understanding of even simple facts. In schools and youth clubs, even in universities and colleges of education, in town or country, in deprived or prosperous areas, young people regularly ask the same questions. The visitor or teacher is expected to fill the gaps in knowledge about physiology and reproduction. The older the child, and the longer such matters are left, the more likely is the youngster to acquire misleading ideas. Instruction will therefore be needed to dispel unreasonable fears and negate old wives' tales.

Although there are many excellent books now available, it is still not easy to prepare suitable lessons or projects for the educationally backward who may be socially sophisticated. Their vocabulary limits the expression of their knowledge and ideas in the classroom. What is needed may be some form of comic strip, with the captions in the language of the homes and streets. Such 'literature' would no doubt be banned from school, yet the teacher must be aware of the conflicts in the child's mind and seek to resolve them by using appropriate words, and translating them if necessary. Technical terms and complicated diagrams presented in the classroom, often drive a wedge between the facts and their application to the child's own feelings.

Questions arise even when human reproduction has no place on the timetable. English, History, Bible study, stories of people in other lands, even simple story-telling, all such subjects may lead to questions about love and marriage, the birth of babies, the care of children. Family life, quarrels, infidelity, divorce, all personal relationships, are as much a part of our history as wars and conquest. For the backward child, concrete instances and examples teach more effectively than abstract principles, and therefore stories, illustrations, drama, 'The doing of life' (Slade), are useful methods. The keeping of pets is widely encouraged and the differences as well as the similarities of animal and human behaviour may be emphasized, especially because of the need for prolonged care. Caring for others might be the dominant theme of all teaching of personal relationships.

Such a theme is surely the basis of our welfare state, and knowledge about the self paves the way to the understanding of others and the need for cooperation. Young people during their school life gradually learn to weaken the emotional bonds with parents. Through social life in school with friends and teachers, with gangs of like-minded children, and less happy relationships with enemies, children change their attitudes. Enemies of one term become the friends of the next and eventually a personal identity emerges. It is during these changing periods of life that rules are sought. No longer the rules that apply because 'father says so' or 'mother or teacher would get angry', but an understanding of 'the Law' becomes important. True, for some the only rule is not to get caught, while for others, rules are only to be broken; but for the majority, the law gives important guidance beyond the parental prohibitions. Lessons on the subject are of great interest since they affect us in all our commercial transactions, which we now undertake on our own responsibility at eighteen; and changing laws affect profoundly our habits and ways of thinking about such matters as marriage and divorce, family planning and abortion, homosexuality and prostitution, child care and protection, industrial and racial relationships.

Apart from the law, it is the individual integrity and capacity of loving relationships that really determine the pattern of life, whether in family, friendship or at work. Caring and responsible relationships make for stable communities based on stable families. The teacher can only hope to be sensitive in the area of feelings and glean from what the children say, their deeper needs. Boys and girls will test the teacher's tolerance, resilience, humour and shockability to the limit, but behind the remarks and questions, designed to show off, or for a giggle, there may be a truly worried child.

Straightforward information should be designed to reassure, to comfort, and above all, to bring hope to damaged children, through the search for truth.

Academic backwardness need not always involve social or emotional retardation, and in time, any child may grow up to be a reliable and happy member of the community. I well remember a backward, immigrant boy showing me his model of a space-ship and relating his story of the crew who would find a planet far away where people do not hate and fight one another. Surely this is the eternal longing, and the end for which all education should be devised.

We have seen that Education for Personal Relationships is not just a subject for 'chalk and talk' nor is it a euphemism for sex education. It is a carefully considered use of the talents of a team of teachers to promote social and emotional growth in their pupils. The young child is helped in the remedial class to accept himself and make the best possible adjustment to his handicaps. The older child is guided through social situations requiring interaction with others. He learns through the inevitable trials and errors to cope with rivalry, envy and competition as he gains the sense of achievement and the rewards of hard work and cooperation.

In group-work structured to promote good relationships, spontaneous questions and discussions are encouraged, since young people learn much from each other. Visiting counsellors encounter questions such as those given below. They are mainly concerned with sex because the subject has not usually been adequately covered by teachers or parents and because the relationships with the opposite sex become the dominant theme at this age. The questions come from a cross-section of boys and girls in ordinary and approved schools and reflect the wide variety of literacy and maturity among children of the same age. Spelling has been corrected.

SOME TYPICAL QUESTIONS FROM FOURTEEN-YEAR-OLD BOYS AND GIRLS.

Why don't parents tell us?

Do you think it right for parents to tell their young children the true facts of life rather than that they were found under gooseberry bushes?

Who does one turn to if one's parents are too shy?

Parents don't let you tell anything you have on your mind, so you find advice from other people. This makes the relationship not so close.

During a conversation, my brother, eight-years-old, asked me where babies come from, before the mother. I explained briefly about eggs fusing, one from the mother of the child and one from the father. He asked how this happened. I told him to ask mother, he didn't. In this instance I evaded the question. How could I have dealt with the subject without frightening him or confusing it with the lavatory which he is particularly preoccupied with at the moment?

What causes a woman's monthly period?

How is the breast prepared for feeding? Do the nipples open?

Are sex organs very delicate things?

How are triplets and quads formed?

What is the right age to have a baby?

How can I tell my parents that I want to go out and meet people? I always have to be home by 8 o'clock and I am sent to bed with my younger sister.

I want to be free but I dare not tell my parents.

What time should a 14-year-old girl or boy be in at night?

How can you prevent a trusted friend from turning against you?

How does one recognise a 'nice' boy?

What should you do and what should you say when a girl wants to go out with you and you do not want to? How should you break it off?

How should a girl act on her first date?

What age should we be allowed to go with boys?

How many times a week should a school girl go out in the evening?

I am not interested in girls. Will I get over this?

How can you overcome shyness towards girls you have never met or spoken to?

How can one stop being shy when with boys?

Do you have to sleep with a man to become pregnant?

Do you think girls expect sex when they are out with boys and are boys expected to do this?

What can you do when you are out with a girl and she asks you a question that will embarrass you?

How many times a week should you go out and what should you do?

What would you do if your girl was going with someone else?

What can you do if your parents think you are too young to go with boys?

At what age can boys become homosexual?

What is a love bite? Why is it a status symbol?

Is it normal for men and women to masturbate on their own?

Is it true that bosoms get bigger through handling?

How far should you let a boy go?

I have heard of many unpleasant doings when a boy is with a girl. Are they necessary?

Do drugs make you feel sexy?

Please could you tell me the best way to explain your emotional feelings to a girl?

How would you know if you had chosen the right girl friend and what would you look for?

I thought sex was to do with male and female but when men and women have children why do they call it sex? What does sex mean?

If a girl is frightened of sex what would you advise her to do about it?

Why does sperm fertilise human eggs?

If there is no hymen has she had intercourse?

Explain sexual intercourse.

Could you tell us about how you go about getting to know girls better, if they are interested in sex and you are, but you don't know how to go about it?

What happens if the girl asks you for intercourse?

Do you think that sex before marriage is wrong?

Does sex hurt the male as much as the female?

How does one know what to do on one's wedding night?

What is it advisable to do if you find your girl friend is pregnant?

Is a boy of 20 too old for a girl of 14? How far should we go and how do we persuade parents it is all right?

Do you think you should have sex before or after marriage for the first time?

How should I go about to ask a girl to marry me?

Do you have to pay fees for a wedding?

How would I set about having children when I get older and get married?

What is V.D.?

Can you catch V.D. from kissing?

Should girls take the birth-pill?

Is it right to take the pill and why?

Is it safe to use Durex or does it still leave a risk?
Is it true that you can give yourself a miscarriage by drinking a lot of alcohol?
How dangerous is abortion?
What do you think of 'Groupies'?
Should mixed marriages take place?
When people divorce why do they do it? What does the other person think?
Why do people row? Why can't they get a divorce?
What should we do if a marriage goes wrong?

In discussion one finds that behind the giggling and hesitancy, no matter what the social background, there is a keen desire for honest explanation of the facts, a search for guidance in personal conduct and a concern for moral values.

REFERENCES

A. G. Chanter: *Sex education in the Primary school.* Macmillan, 1966.
A. Clegg and B. Megson: *Children in distress.* Penguin, 1968.
J. Dawkins: *A textbook of sex education.* Basil Blackwell, 1967.
R. Hacker: *Telling the teenagers.* Deutsch, 1966.
R. Hacker: *Health and happiness (The Working World).* Cassell, 1967.
15–18 : Crowther Report, 1959. *Half our future :* Newsom Report, 1963.
Cross'd with adversity : Working Paper, 1970. H.M.S.O.
A. Jones: *School counselling in prəctice.* Ward Lock Educational, 1969.
Young people in relationship : book list from National Marriage Guidance Council.
S. Segal: *No child is uneducable.* Pergamon Press, 1967.
M. Schofield: *The sexual behaviour of young people.* Longmans, 1965, Penguin, 1970.
P. Slade: *Child drama.* University of London Press, 1954.
A. E. Tansley and R. Gulliford: *The education of slow learning children.* Routledge, 1960.
The Humanities Curriculum Project. Heinemann Educational Books.

Index

Printed in Great Britain by
Cox & Wyman Limited
London, Fakenham and Reading